CLOCK JACKS AND BEE BOLES

Courtney Dainton

WITH TWENTY-THREE PLATES
BY THE AUTHOR

Fire hooks in the parish church, Iver, Buckinghamshire

CLOCK JACKS
AND
BEE BOLES

✦➤✦➤✦➤✦➤✦➤✦➤✦➤✦➤✦

A Dictionary of Country Sights by

Courtney Dainton

PHOENIX HOUSE LTD
LONDON

75955

Printed in Great Britain
in 9/11 point Monotype Times Roman by
Wyman & Sons Ltd.,
London, Reading and Fakenham, for
Phoenix House Ltd., 38 William IV Street,
Charing Cross, W.C.2

First published 1957

TO MY
FATHER AND MOTHER

Illustrations

Preface

ALTHOUGH there is an abundance of books on the works of nature—trees, grasses, wild flowers, animals, birds and insects—there appears to be no concise guide to the many interesting works of man which one comes across when travelling through the British countryside. This book is an attempt to make good this deficiency and to enable those who love the countryside to add even more enjoyment to their journeys.

Every effort has been made to ensure that the book is as complete as possible, but this task has been so difficult that I fear readers will think of other subjects which should have been included. When the work was commenced I myself had no idea that there are so many objects worthy of note.

It should be pointed out that churches, other religious buildings such as monasteries, and castles, have been omitted deliberately because there is already a vast literature dealing with them and there are usually adequate accounts of them in the ordinary guidebooks. Descriptions have, however, been included of many of the more unusual objects found in churches, such as acoustic jars, dumb borsholders, and sextons' wheels, since the guidebooks often fail even to mention these. Wherever possible, particulars are given of one or two books from which fuller information regarding the objects can be obtained.

C. D

CLOCK JACKS AND BEE BOLES

A DICTIONARY OF COUNTRY SIGHTS

A

Acoustic Jar. Acoustic jars were a form of amplifier used in churches in the Middle Ages. They look like earthenware pitchers lying on their sides with their open mouths pointing into the church. A number of these jars were embedded in the chancel walls in order to add resonance to the voices of the priest and the choir. Today less than half-a-dozen churches still possess acoustic jars; they include St Clement's at Sandwich in Kent and Barkway church in Hertfordshire.

Act of Parliament Clock. Sometimes a clock in the entrance hall of an old inn is called an Act of Parliament clock because it is supposed to be placed there in continuance of a practice commenced in 1797, when clocks and watches were taxed and many people ceased to carry watches. Some people think that this explanation is incorrect and that the clocks were provided for the benefit of people travelling by the stage-coaches which used inns as halting places. Since an Act of Parliament clock does not differ in appearance from any ordinary clock, it is a little difficult to understand why it should have been given a special name at all.

Aerial Ferry. See *Transporter Bridge*

Alignment. This usually consists of parallel rows of stones, which often lead to a stone circle or ancient sanctuary. It may also be an earthwork without stones. A good example of a stone avenue leads to the circle at Avebury, Wiltshire. As in the case of the circles, the purpose for which the avenues were erected is unknown, but they probably date from the Bronze Age. There are a number of stone rows on Dartmoor; in some cases there are ancient burial chambers between the stones.

Almshouse. Almshouses are charitable institutions where accommodation is provided, usually for the aged and infirm. They originated in the Middle Ages, when they were usually known as hospitals. Some of them still retain this name; others are called colleges.

Many almshouses were founded in the twelfth and thirteenth centuries and often they were provided with a trained staff to care for the inmates. Later, the system changed and the almshouses were used as accommodation for people who, though aged, were capable of looking after themselves.

Archbishops and bishops were responsible for the establishment of a large number of almshouses. Among their foundations which still function today are St John's Hospital, Canterbury (founded about 1084 by Archbishop Lanfranc) and St Cross Hospital, Winchester (founded about 1133 by Bishop Henry de Blois). St Cross Hospital is one of the almshouses where the inmates wear a distinctive uniform. In the case of St Cross, there are two uniforms; men belonging to the original foundation wear a black gown and a badge in the form of a silver cross, while the members of the foundation of Cardinal Beaufort, who re-established the hospital in 1445, wear a red gown and have as their symbol a cardinal's hat embroidered on it in white.

Some almshouses disappeared at the Reformation, but many new ones were founded. Wealthy churchmen ceased to be so prominent among the benefactors and their place was taken by wealthy laymen. Sometimes these benefactors made it a condition of their endowment that the inmates of their almshouse should belong to a certain sect, a certain trade, or come from a certain locality. For example, in 1622 some almshouses were erected at Godalming, Surrey, in accordance with the will of Richard Wyatt, who stipulated that they should provide lodgings for five poor men from Godalming, two from Puttenham, and one each from the other neighbouring villages of Hambledon, Compton, and Dunsfold.

The exact number of almshouses in England is not known,

but it has been estimated that there are about 2,500 and that they provide homes for about 50,000 people. There are always plenty of applicants for accommodation in them and it seems that these old institutions will continue to serve a useful purpose for many years to come.

(See also *Bede House*)

The Medieval Hospitals of England, by R. M. Clay (Methuen, 1909)

The English Almshouse, by W. H. Godfrey (Faber, 1955)

Ancient Lights. These words on the wall of a building indicate that the owner has the right to receive an uninterrupted flow of light at one or more of the windows without obstruction. This right may have originated either by a grant or by twenty years' uninterrupted enjoyment of the light, on the presumption that such enjoyment has always existed. Such a right can be acquired only in respect of a building, and not in connection with open land. If the owner of a building which possesses the right to ancient lights enlarges the windows, he can take no action against anybody obstructing the enlargements, unless they also obstruct the original windows.

Ancient Trackway, or **Green Road.** The earliest man-made tracks were probably developed by the people of the New Stone Age (2500–1900 B.C.). The tracks were the means of communication between one small community and the next; they were used by the people of the settlements when they engaged in barter, the earliest form of trade. At first the men trod the tracks carrying their goods upon their backs, but later pack-horses were used.

Usually the roads ran along the hill-tops, where the travellers felt safer from attack. Journeying was easier on the hills, too, for much of the lowland was covered with forests and swamps.

It was not only trade which led to the making of trackways, for in the south of England many of the roads converged at the important religious centre of Avebury, in Wiltshire, the site of the largest stone circle in Britain. Of course, many of the people made one journey serve two purposes, so that Avebury was also the scene of much trading.

The course of the tracks was marked by mounds, some of which were used for burials, while others appear to have been made in order to mark the route and guide travellers. Such signposts were undoubtedly very necessary, for in times of heavy rainfall or snowfall the tracks would become indistinguishable from the surrounding countryside.

Hill forts, such as Maiden Castle, near Dorchester, were constructed along the trade routes. Their purpose was not only defensive; they, too, were important trading centres.

Today many of these ancient tracks can still be traced for miles across the countryside. They include the famous Pilgrims' Way along the North Downs, which was used long before Thomas à Becket was murdered at Canterbury; the Ridgeway in Berkshire; and the Icknield Way in East Anglia.

The Green Roads of England, by R. Hippisley Cox (Methuen, 1914)

Anglian Cross. See *High Cross*

Aqueduct. An aqueduct is an artificial channel or conduit for conveying water. Usually it is an elevated structure which carries water across a valley.

Aqueducts were built by the Romans, but the first modern aqueduct in Britain was that constructed by James Brindley at Burton, Lancashire, to carry the Bridgewater Canal over the River Irwell. When the Manchester Ship Canal was built, Brindley's structure was replaced by a swing aqueduct.

Another great canal engineer, Thomas Telford, was responsible for the construction of a number of fine aqueducts. The most important of these is undoubtedly the Pont-Cysylltau aqueduct, near Chirk in Shropshire. It carries the Ellesmere Canal across the River Dee; it is over 1,000 feet long and is 127 feet above the river.

Art Gallery. It was not until the nineteenth century that buildings were opened where the public could see the work of

Aqueduct carrying the Kennet and Avon canal over the river Avon and the railway at Avoncliff, Wiltshire

Cauldron, Frensham, Surrey

Jacobean chest, Warfield, Berkshire

famous artists. Previously the only art collections were in the private houses of wealthy people. Now most cities and large towns have an art gallery; often it is in the same building as the museum.

Because of the large expense involved in forming and maintaining a collection of pictures, very few small towns or villages have art galleries. There are, however, two village galleries worthy of mention. One is at Compton in Surrey, where paintings by the famous Victorian artist G. F. Watts are exhibited; he lived in the village for many years. The other is at Ashford-in-the-Water in Derbyshire, where an enthusiastic local lady has converted a derelict tithe barn into an art gallery.

Artificial Mound. The men of the Bronze Age were great builders, and their best works are to be found in one county, Wiltshire. There, besides erecting the great sanctuaries of Avebury and Stonehenge, they also built the largest artificial mound in Europe. It is Silbury Hill, about a mile from Avebury; it is 120 feet high and its base has a circumference of 450 feet. The purpose for which this mound was erected has never been ascertained. Most mounds are usually much smaller and were burial places, but if there is a grave beneath Silbury Hill it still remains to be discovered.

Ash House, or **Joanna House.** In that part of Dartmoor which lies between Chagford and Widecombe there are a number of farmhouses which have near them a small granite building with a domed roof. Most of these structures are circular, with a diameter of about seven feet; a few of them are square. Up to about eighty years ago they were used for the storage of ashes scraped from fireplaces and ovens. On the side of the building nearest the farmhouse there is an iron hatch through which the ashes were tipped; on the opposite side there is an iron door. The ashes were mixed with poultry manure and used as a fertilizer for root crops.

Since the quantity of root crops grown in this area is small, it seems probable that the storage of ashes for this purpose was only a secondary consideration. The main object was to

B

reduce the danger of fire caused by sparks lighting the thatch with which at that time most farmhouses were roofed.

B

Badger Pit. One of the cruel sports in which countrymen used to take delight was badger baiting. This took place in a small pit, six or seven feet wide and a foot or two feet deep. The pit was surrounded by a wall about five feet high and on the outside of this wall there was a small platform on which the spectators stood.

A tiny tunnel leading into the pit formed the badger's refuge. The poor animal was placed in the pit together with a dog, and wagers were laid on the number of times the dog would manage to make the badger come out of the tunnel. When the badger came from the tunnel into the pit, the animals were kept apart by some suitable instrument, such as a shovel.

Badger baiting was made illegal in the middle of the nineteenth century and few badger pits remain. There is one at Braziers Park near Ipsden in Oxfordshire.

Bakehouse. Some remote villages used to have a communal bakehouse, where all the inhabitants baked their bread. A few of these bakehouses remain; they are usually very small buildings with very tall chimneys. There is one at Papworth St Agnes in Huntingdonshire.

Bargain Stone. A bargain stone was sometimes to be found in market places. When a man wished to buy from a merchant he placed his money on the stone; this indicated that the contract was sealed.

There are bargain stones at Barnstaple in Devon, and at Retford in Nottinghamshire. That at Barnstaple is a flat round stone on a pedestal; it is kept on the site of the town's old quay, where the merchants gathered to transact their business.

Barrel-organ. The modern manual organ did not come into use until about a hundred and fifty years ago, and before that the music in some churches was provided by barrel-organs. The barrels of these instruments were studded with metal pins; as the barrels were turned the pins opened the pipes and so produced the notes. A few churches still preserve their old organs; there is one at Piddinghoe in Sussex.

Barrow. See *Long Barrow* and *Round Barrow*

Bascule Bridge. This is a type of movable bridge in which the moving portion turns vertically about a pivot and rises until the opening is left clear, so that vessels can pass through. The part which moves may be in the form of a single leaf, as in a wooden bridge on the Shropshire Union Canal at Vron Cysyllte, near Llangollen, or a double leaf, as in the best-known of all bascule bridges—London's Tower Bridge.

Beacon. Many hilltops and other high points in the country-side have had fires lit upon them at various times in our history to signal the news of important events. One of these events was, of course, the arrival of the Spanish Armada, and Macaulay, in a well-known poem, listed the sites of some of the beacons. The Scots used beacons as a warning of the approach of the English in the days when the two countries were frequently at war. In 1455 the Scottish Parliament made a law that one fire should be lit as a sign that the English were believed to be on the way, two fires when it was certain that they were coming, and four fires if they were advancing in great numbers.

Some of the hills where fires were lit have the word *beacon* as part of their name. Inkpen Beacon in Berkshire, Ivinghoe Beacon in Hertfordshire, and Dunkery Beacon in Somerset are examples of this.

In recent times, when there have been more efficient ways of spreading news, fires have often blazed on the old sites as part of the celebrations of jubilees or coronations. Sometimes a commemorative stone has been placed on the spot where the fires were lit. A stone on the top of Brent Knoll in Somerset has an inscription informing those who reach the summit that fires blazed there at the jubilees of Queen Victoria in 1887 and 1897, and at the coronations of 1902 and 1911.

Bede House. This was an almshouse where the inmates prayed for their benefactors. Some almshouses, such as those at Melton Mowbray in Leicestershire and at Liddington in Rutland are still known as bede houses. (See *Almshouse*)

Bee Bole, or **Bee Hole.** The present type of beehive was not introduced into Britain until 1862. Before that date the straw skep was used, and in order to shelter this from the weather it was often kept in a recess built into a wall. There seems to have been no name in general use in England for this recess, although in parts of Yorkshire it was known as a bee hole; in Scotland, however, it was commonly called a bee bole.

The National Beekeeping Museum opened a register of bee boles in 1952, and within two years over a hundred sets of boles were reported. Of these, seventy-four are in England, thirty-six in Scotland, four in Wales, and three in Ireland. Thirty of the English sets are in Yorkshire, and there are only about ten in the two-thirds of the country which receives less than thirty inches of rain annually.

Most of the boles are in garden or orchard walls, but a few are in walls of houses. They are usually in sets of from two to eight, although at Packwood House, a National Trust property in Warwickshire, there are thirty.

The majority of the boles are between 18 and 30 inches high and between 15 and 28 inches wide. The usual height of the base above the ground is from 18 to 30 inches.

It is very difficult to ascertain the date when any bole was constructed, but some appear to have been built in the fifteenth century. They were widely used in the seventeenth and eighteenth centuries and it is possible that two of the sets sheltered skeps until about 1920.

English Bee Boles, by R. M. Durwz and E. E. Crane (Bee Research Association, 1954)

Beehive Hut, or **Hutment.** This is the name given to the site of the hut constructed by a Stone Age man. Usually only a round depression in the ground marks the site, but sometimes there are stones at the circumference. The finest group is at Chysauster in Cornwall; the best example of a single hut is at Bosporthennis in the same county. The Bosporthennis hut has two chambers, one circular and the other rectangular, the circular chamber having a circumference of about forty feet.

Belfry. Originally a belfry was a tower erected for defensive purposes. Later the name was applied to a building from which an alarm bell was rung, and then it came to denote a bell-tower —usually one attached to ecclesiastical buildings.

Most belfries form part of the church to which they belong, but occasionally they are separate buildings, as at Beccles, Berkeley, and Evesham. The only cathedral with a separate belfry is that at Chichester.

There are a few non-ecclesiastical belfries. St Albans has one which was built in the fifteenth century, and there are others at Morpeth in Northumberland, at Glasgow, and at Aberdeen.

Bell Barrow. See *Round Barrow*

Bench Mark. A bench mark consists of a broad arrow with a horizontal line along the top. It indicates that the Ordnance Survey Office has ascertained the exact height of the spot above sea-level, which is the mean level of the sea at Newlyn in Cornwall. It takes its name from a surveyor's angle iron, which he uses as a ' bench ' or support for his levelling staff. Bench marks are found on a variety of convenient objects, such as walls, pillars, and gate-posts.

Blind House. See *Lock-up*

Blind Window. In 1696 the government levied a tax on windows. The owners of all inhabited houses, except those not paying church or poor rates, had to pay two shillings a year. There was also an additional tax based on the number of windows in the house.

This measure led to the blocking-up of many windows. In some cases they were replaced with plain stone, but in others representations of the windows—black panes and white frames —were painted on the outside walls. These paintings were known as blind windows, and quite a number of them still remain.

The window-tax was not repealed until 1851.

Blow Well. This is a reservoir of artesian well water. It takes the form of a deep pit of water, and often people living in the locality attempt to spread the belief that it is bottomless. There are several blow wells near Tetney in Lincolnshire.

Boundary Cross. See *Sanctuary Cross*

Bowl Barrow. See *Round Barrow*

Brank. See *Gossip's Bridle*

Bread Rack. Hanging on the wall of the church at Milton Ernest in Bedfordshire is a bread rack with pigeon-holes for twelve loaves. It dates from 1729, when a local inhabitant left money to provide poor people with twelve loaves each week. This charity is still carried out.

(See also *Dole Cupboard*)

Bridal Door. The churches of Lydd and Tenterden in Kent both possess at their west ends double doors known as bridal doors. One was intended for the bride and the other for the bridegroom.

Bridge. The earliest form of bridge was a tree which had fallen across a stream. Man followed Nature's example and deliberately felled trees so that they bridged streams. It was but a short step from the tree bridge to the bridge consisting of a single slab of stone resting on other stones at each end. This type is known as the clam bridge, of which several examples still exist; there is one at Wycoller in Lancashire.

After the clam bridge came the clapper bridge, consisting of several slabs instead of only one. Wycoller also possesses one of these, but the best-known examples are probably Post Bridge on Dartmoor and Tarr Steps on Exmoor.

The clapper bridge remained the most elaborate type this country could produce until the Romans arrived. So little remains of Roman bridges, however, that it seems certain they were built of timber. At Chollerford in Northumberland there are the foundations of a Roman bridge.

The Anglo-Saxon bridges were also of timber. The first stone bridge across the Thames was constructed at London in 1209.

Gradually timber bridges were replaced by stone structures. Much of this replacement took place in the fifteenth century. The monasteries were responsible for the erection of many bridges, on some of which small chapels were built where the traveller could pray for a safe journey. Only three of these chapels still exist: at St Ives in Huntingdonshire, and at Rotherham and Wakefield in Yorkshire. There is a bridge chapel at Derby, but the bridge to which it belonged has been replaced by another structure on a slightly different site. Bradford-on-Avon in Wiltshire has a bridge with a tiny oratory on it, the only one of its kind still in existence.

In addition to the monasteries, other bodies which undertook the erection of bridges were the corporations of towns and cities. Some landowners constructed bridges on their estates.

The dissolution of the monasteries led to the passing in 1530 of an Act of Parliament which empowered justices of the peace to ensure that bridges were properly maintained and to levy a rate to meet the cost of their repair.

Some medieval bridges were fortified. The best example still remaining is at Monmouth; it has an elaborate gateway, with openings above the archway from which the defenders could pour boiling tar upon their attackers.

A number of medieval bridges, including London Bridge, had houses built on them. The only medieval housed bridge remaining is High Bridge at Lincoln; Pulteney Bridge at Bath, which also has houses on it, was built in 1770.

The seventeenth century did not see any remarkable bridge-building activity, but in the second half of the eighteenth century the Industrial Revolution, with its demand for improved communications, brought striking developments. One of the most important of these was the construction in 1779 of the world's first iron bridge at Coalbrookdale in Shropshire. This bridge still spans the Severn.

The end of the eighteenth century and the beginning of the nineteenth century witnessed the replacement of the architect bridge-builder by the engineer bridge-builder. Great engineers like John Rennie and Thomas Telford erected bridges which brought them nation-wide fame. Rennie's masterpiece in this sphere was his London Bridge, which replaced the structure of 1209. Telford made great use of iron; his structures include the Menai and Conway suspension bridges.

After iron came steel, which made possible such structures as the Forth Bridge. Steel has been followed by concrete, first in its simple form, and then reinforced with steel. The first concrete bridge in England, at Seaton in Devon, was opened in 1887. London's Waterloo Bridge is a fine example of the use of reinforced concrete.

The Bridges of Britain, by Eric de Maré (Batsford, 1954)

The Ancient Bridges of the South of England, by E. Jervoise (The Architectural Press, 1930)

The Ancient Bridges of the North of England, by E. Jervoise (The Architectural Press, 1931)

The Ancient Bridges of Mid and Eastern England, by E. Jervoise (The Architectural Press, 1932)

See also, in this book, the descriptions of various types of bridges under the following headings: *Bascule bridge; Bucket bridge; Cantilever bridge; Clam bridge; Clapper bridge; Devil's bridge; Military bridge; Movable bridge; Packhorse bridge; Palladian bridge; Suspension bridge; Swing bridge; Transporter bridge; Tubular bridge; War bridge*

Bridge Chapel. See *Bridge*

Bridlepath, or **Bridleway.** This was the name given to a track which was too narrow for carts to use. Today few bridlepaths are used by horses; most of them are now footpaths.

Broch. In the Orkney and Shetland Isles there are the remains of nearly two hundred brochs. These are circular defensive towers which were built either by the Picts or by earlier inhabitants. They are constructed of slabs of clay-slate. Their walls are between 15 and 20 feet thick and there are stairs and chambers within this thickness. Inside the broch is a courtyard; the diameter of this varies from 20 feet to 40 feet. There is only one small entrance, near which are two cells, probably sleeping quarters, and a guard-room. A stairway winds from the bottom to the top of the building, and corridors branch off from this stairway. Openings in the inner wall served as windows to admit light to the stairs and the corridors. The lower part of the outer wall slopes inwards, becoming perpendicular when it reaches a height of about 25 feet.

The construction of these brochs involved a tremendous amount of labour, for each one contained at least five thousand tons of stone. The best-preserved broch, at Mousa in the Shetlands, is still 45 feet high.

Bronze Age Sanctuary. Britain's most famous prehistoric monument is Stonehenge, a temple or sanctuary of the Bronze Age. This type of monument is sometimes called an embanked sanctuary because it consists of a circle of stones surrounded by a ditch, which, in its turn, is enclosed by an embankment. It is this ditch inside the embankment which shows that the monument was erected for religious and not for military purposes: if the ditch had been intended as a measure of defence, it would be on the outside.

The embankment at Stonehenge is not very pronounced, but at another sanctuary at Avebury, also in Wiltshire, it is quite imposing. There are two smaller stone circles inside the main circle at Avebury, whereas Stonehenge consists of a double outer circle with a horseshoe of stones inside it.

The number of entrances in the embankment of this type of sanctuary varied; there may have been one, two, or four. The material used to form the circle also varied: sometimes there were wooden posts instead of stone pillars. Only the stones have survived, of course, although the sites of some wooden circles are known. One of them has been discovered and marked out at Woodhenge, only a few miles from Stonehenge.

There has been a great deal of discussion regarding the purpose for which these temples were erected, and whether there was any astronomical significance in their design. Stonehenge, in particular, has been the subject of numerous books.

A Guide to the Prehistoric and Roman Monuments in England and Wales, by Jacquetta Hawkes (Chatto and Windus, 1951)

Bucket Bridge. This rare type of bridge consists of a wooden box suspended on a steel cable and propelled by ropes and pulleys. There is a bucket bridge in Glen Orchy in Argyllshire; here seats are provided in the box, which is reached by climbing a flight of wooden steps.

Bull Ring. The barbarous sport of bull-baiting was popular for at least six centuries and was not made illegal until 1835. The sport consisted of a duel between a bulldog and a bull. The bull had a collar round its neck to which a chain was fastened. The other end of the chain was attached to a ring which was fixed to a post. So that the bull could move round to face an attack from any direction, the chain was connected to the ring by a swivel.

The bulldog endeavoured to seize the bull's nose and hold on to it. The bull, of course, tried to prevent this, usually by putting his nose in a hole in the ground. If the dog failed to hold on to the bull, he was often tossed into the air, and the force of his fall frequently killed him.

There are still a few bull-rings left; one is at Loppington in Shropshire.

The village of Leslie in Fifeshire has another type of bull-baiting relic known as a bull stone. It is a stone on the village green to which the bull was tethered. Round the stone there is a groove worn by the chain used to hold the bull.

Buried Church. There are a few churches which were once buried; a few of them are still partly buried now. Encroaching sand has been chiefly responsible for the entombments. Churches which used to be under the sand can be found at three places in Cornwall—Perranzabuloe, Rock, and St Enodoc. Inland, buried churches are extremely rare; there is the crypt—all that remains—of one of these at Chilton Candover in Hampshire.

Butter Cross. This name is occasionally given to a market cross (q.v.). Bingham in Nottinghamshire possesses a butter cross which is also a memorial cross, since it was erected in memory of a local worthy. The butter cross at Witney in Oxfordshire was built in 1683; it has a gabled roof supported by thirteen stone columns.

C

Cage. See *Lock-up*

Cairn. In stone country cairns were often erected over burials of the Early and Middle Bronze Ages (1900-1000 B.C.), instead of the barrows so common in the south of England. The men of the Iron Age (450 B.C. to A.D. 43) also erected cairns, sometimes forming a cemetery of them. There is one of these cemeteries on Danby High Moor in Yorkshire.

Campanile. This is a detached bell-tower or belfry (q.v.). The name is also sometimes used to denote a clock-tower.

Canal. Canals are artificial waterways, constructed for the purpose of providing means of navigation, either by connecting two rivers or else running parallel to a river which is not navigable. A ship canal is a canal built to convert an inland town into a seaport or to give old ports access to the sea.

Two great problems facing engineers were water supply and changes in the level of the land through which the canal passed. Where a canal is parallel to a river it obtains its water supply from the river; a canal joining two rivers may get its water from streams above the level of the canal, but often this supply is insufficient and reservoirs have to be constructed, or water may have to be pumped to the canal from springs or wells at a lower level.

The most common method of overcoming differences in the level of the land is by locks. A lock can be likened to a chamber with a gate at each end. If a boat is ascending, the water in the chamber must be level with that in the canal below the lock. The boat enters the chamber and the gate is locked. The sluices on the upper gate are then opened and the chamber fills with water, so that the boat is raised to the level of the water in the upper section, which it then enters.

Certain lifting devices, such as the vertical lift, are sometimes used in place of locks. There is only one vertical lift now in use—the Anderton Lift, which raises and lowers boats through a height of 50 feet between the River Weaver and the Trent and Mersey Canal.

The first canal in this country was made by the Romans. It is Foss Dyke, which runs from Lincoln to Torksey, and it is still in use. After the departure of the Romans more than a thousand years elapsed before another canal was constructed. In the reign of Elizabeth I the Exeter Ship Canal was built. It was not until the second half of the eighteenth century that the Duke of Bridgewater inaugurated the canal era when he employed James Brindley, the engineer, to construct a canal from Worsley to Barton. The Duke spent the greater part of his large fortune in this work, the purpose of which was to convey coal from his collieries to Manchester. However, he soon made a handsome profit, and others were not slow to try to follow his example. The great canal boom had begun.

The canal era lasted until the coming of the railways. During this period about three thousand miles of canal were constructed; of these, less than two thousand miles are now available for navigation. The longest canal is the Grand Union Canal, which has a total length of 300 miles; there are two canals only half a mile long.

Many canals have fallen into disuse, often as a result of the policy deliberately followed by the early railway companies, who bought the canals so that they should not compete with the railways. When the railways were nationalized, these canals passed into the control of the British Transport Commission. The Commission have made some improvements, but are seeking authority to abandon many miles of canals. Opposition to this step is being organized by the Inland Waterways Association, who consider that far greater use should be made of the canals.

British Canals, by Charles Hadfield (Phoenix House, 1950)

The Story of Our Inland Waterways, by Robert Aickman (Pitman, 1955)

The Canals of Southern England, by Charles Hadfield (Phoenix House, 1955)

The Inland Waterways of England, by L. T. C. Rolt (Allen and Unwin, 1950)

Canal Tunnel. One of the earliest canal tunnels was constructed at Harecastle on the Trent and Mersey Canal, which was completed in 1777. It is 2,919 yards long and has no towpath. The barges were propelled through it by men lying on their backs and pushing with their feet against the walls of the tunnel These men were known as 'leggers'. This tunnel cannot now be used because of the subsidence which has taken place.

There is a much longer tunnel on the Huddersfield Canal. It is known as the Standedge Tunnel and is over three miles long.

Candle Hole. In a few churches holes will be found in the tops of the bench-ends. These are believed to have been made for holding candles when the church had no other means of lighting, although there are some people who consider that it was more likely that they were used to hold holly. Such holes can be seen in the church at Minety, in Wiltshire.

Cantilever Bridge. The development of this type of bridge was made possible by the invention of steel. It consists of steel trusses projecting from piers and connected to each other by short spans. The best-known cantilever bridge is, of course, the Forth Bridge, which was completed in 1889. With its approaches, it is over 1½ miles long, and carries two railway tracks 150 feet above the Firth of Forth.

Car Catcher. One or two bridges are fitted with a heavy iron railing to catch any vehicles that happen to fall through the parapet. There is one of these car catchers on a bridge near Llangollen, where the road bends sharply after coming down a steep hill.

Carillon. Strictly speaking a carillon is a set of bells upon which tunes can be played by means of a keyboard mechanism, but often the word is used to describe the tower in which the carillon is housed. The bells are fixed in position and cannot be swung. Another way in which they differ from chimes is in the fact that they are struck on the outside by hammers.

After the 1914-18 War a carillon was erected as a war memorial at Loughborough. There are also carillons at Bournville, Cattistock, and Manchester.

Cattle Chain. Some church porches had a chain attached to the wall. This chain could be stretched across the doorway to prevent cattle straying into the church. Part of such a chain can be seen at Newick in Sussex.

Cauldron. The duties of churchwardens used to be far more numerous and varied than they are today. They included the organization of ' Church ales '—entertainments in which the whole parish participated. For brewing the ale or boiling whole sheep for these feasts they used a large cauldron. One of these cauldrons is preserved in the church at Frensham in Surrey; it is made of copper and is 33 inches wide and 15 inches deep.

Causewayed Camp. There are a number of these embanked enclosures in the south of England consisting of concentric rings of banks and ditches. The minimum number of ditches is two and they are interrupted by causeways formed by leaving the chalk at certain points undisturbed. It is doubtful if these causeways served any purpose. Excavations have shown that sometimes there were fences along the banks and wooden gates at the causeways.

The camps were probably used for a few days each autumn, when the men of the New Stone Age (2500-1900 B.C.) rounded up their cattle before winter set in. This theory is based on the fact that, with one exception, no huts have been found within any of these camps, although the ditches contain plenty of rubbish, such as remains of pottery and meat bones.

The single camp which contained huts was at Hembury, near Honiton in Devonshire. The sites of other causewayed camps can be seen on The Trundle at Goodwood in Sussex; on Knap Hill near Alton Priors in Wiltshire; and on Windmill Hill near Avebury, also in Wiltshire.

Britain B.C., by S. E. Winbolt (Penguin, 1943)
A Guide to the Prehistoric and Roman Monuments in England and Wales, by Jacquetta Hawkes (Chatto and Windus, 1951)

Cave Dwelling. Caves were the dwelling-places of people of the Old and Middle Stone Ages—the period of prehistory prior to 2500 B.C. Even as late as Roman times caves were occasionally used as homes. None of the cave dwellings in Britain contain any paintings on their walls such as those found in some continental caverns, but the fact that they were the homes of our remote ancestors has been revealed by the flint implements and the bones of the animals they ate, which were left on the cave floors. At Wookey Hole, in Somerset, there are caves which were occupied in the Old Stone Age and also some which served as dwellings in the Iron Age (450 B.C. to A.D. 43).

Chained Library. See *Public Library*

Chalk Figure. See *Hill Figure*

Chapel Bridge. See *Bridge*

Chest. Many churches contain chests, usually of wood; some of these are elaborately carved while others are roughly hewn from a single piece of wood. These chests were used to safeguard the parish registers and the churchwardens' accounts, although many of them were made before 1538, the date when the keeping of parish registers was made compulsory. Some were made for use as collecting-boxes, as a result of a decree by the Pope at the end of the twelfth century that every church should have a chest into which parishioners could put contributions towards the cost of the Crusades. Crusading chests can usually be distinguished by the slit in the lid through which money was placed.

The exact age of most chests is unknown, but some have the year in which they were made carved on the lid or on the side. The date of the chest at Ashburton, Devon, is recorded in the parish records, in which it is stated that in 1483 a man was paid sixpence for making the chest.

Most chests were made of oak, but other kinds of wood were also used. Some chests were of iron. The lid of the iron chest at Stonham Aspall, in Suffolk, is so heavy that pulleys have to be used to lift it. The chest at Crondall in Hampshire is made of six layers of material; commencing from the inside, they are leather, plaster of paris, sheet iron, oak, sheet iron again, and then iron bands.

Some of the chests have complicated locking devices. The chest at Bucklebury in Berkshire has nine locks which are all operated by a single turn of the key. The lock of the oak chest at Bosham in Sussex has a bolt which runs the whole length of one side of the chest. A secret chamber is incorporated in this chest; the lid of the chamber is the false bottom of a small box. Another remarkable lock is that of the iron chest at Oxted in Surrey; it covers the whole lid and has thirteen bolts which all shoot together when the key is turned.

The size of the chests varies considerably. Usually they are about four feet long, but that at Aldenham, Herts, which was hollowed out of a piece of solid oak, is ten feet long. It has seventeen hinges.

There are several chests which are believed to have come over in ships of the Spanish Armada; they include those at Brookland and Hythe in Kent, and at Braunton in Devon. The chest at Harty in Kent is thought to have been made in Germany.

Church mark, Cowfold, Sussex

City post, Horton, Buckinghamshire

A folly, South Harting, Sussex

Dolmen, St David's Head, Pembrokeshire

Some chests are still used as collecting-boxes; others still hold the parish records. Some are no longer used for any purpose at all and stand, almost unnoticed, in a corner of the church.

The Parish Chest, by W. E. Tate (Cambridge University Press, 1946)

Ancient Church Chests and Chairs in the Home Counties round Greater London, by F. Roe (Batsford, 1929)

Chimney. Sometimes a solitary chimney stack is seen standing long after the rest of the cottage to which it belonged has disappeared. There are two reasons why the chimney may not have been pulled down. One is that some people believe that the house still exists legally as long as the chimney remains, and this ensures the continuance of certain property rights. The second reason arises from the idea that when people are moving to a new house their family ghost will be detained in its old haunt if a chimney is left standing. This belief used to be particularly strong in Shropshire.

Church Mark. The responsibility for keeping the church property in a good state of repair was often shared amongst the parishioners. In the case of the churchyard fence, the names of the farms whose tenants had to repair it were sometimes carved on the posts. Such names can still be seen on the fence at Cowfold in Sussex.

Churchyard Cross. Some of our oldest churchyard crosses were erected long before the churches near which they stand. They were set up as preaching crosses by early Christian missionaries, often on or near the sites of pagan shrines. Some of them are ornately carved. Derbyshire possesses three good examples— at Eyam, Bakewell, and Teddington. That at Teddington is probably six or seven hundred years older than the church, which dates from the fourteenth century. Some churchyards have several crosses; there are three at both Ilkley in Yorkshire and at Whalley in Lancashire. Two of those at Whalley acted for a long time as gateposts; probably their use for this

C

purpose commenced during the time of the Puritans, when many churchyard crosses were destroyed or mutilated.

(See also *Preaching Cross*)

Old Crosses and Lych-gates, by Aymer Vallance (Batsford, 1920)

Churchyard Stable. A stable is an unusual building to find in a churchyard, but at Wixford in Warwickshire there is a wooden stable with a thatched roof. This was provided for the vicar's horse. Wixford did not have a vicar of its own and the services were taken by the clergyman from a neighbouring village, who left his horse in the stable while he was carrying out his duties.

Circle. See *Cromlech*

City Post. In 1861 an Act of Parliament was passed authorizing the Corporation of the City of London to charge duties on wine and coal coming into London. The money obtained in this way was to be used for road improvements. To indicate the points at which these duties were payable, posts bearing the arms of the City of London and the inscription *Act* 24 & 25 *Vict. Cap* 42 were erected at the boundaries of the Metropolitan Police District. A number of these stones can be seen on Walton Heath and at several other places.

Clam Bridge. This is the oldest type of bridge, apart from that formed by a tree-trunk. It consists of a single unhewn slab of stone. Several clam bridges still exist; there is one at Wycoller in Lancashire and another on Dartmoor. The Wycoller bridge is about ten feet long, and the reason for its erection is a mystery for it does not form part of any road or track.

Clapper Bridge. This is a primitive type of bridge, consisting of large slabs of stone resting on stone piers. Well-known clapper bridges are Post Bridge on Dartmoor and Tarr Steps on Exmoor. The latter was washed away in the floods of 1952, but has been rebuilt. There are also clapper bridges at Wycoller in Lancashire, at Linton in Yorkshire, and at several places in Gloucestershire.

Clapper Gate. See *Gate*

Clergy House. Only a few clergy houses or priests' houses, the predecessors of vicarages and rectories, are left. They date from the fourteenth, fifteenth, and sixteenth centuries and were built near the church so that the priest could reach the church easily in order to conduct services, which were far more numerous then than they are today.

The clergy house at Alfriston, in Sussex, which was built about 1350, was the first building to be acquired by the National Trust; it was bought by that body in 1896. It is a simple structure of wattle and daub, with a thatched roof and a clay floor.

Sussex possesses another priest's house at West Hoathly. Built in the same century as that at Alfriston, it is now used as a museum.

Clink. See *Lock-up*

Clock. Only very brief details of the long history of the clock can be given here. The ancient Egyptians used a shadow clock—a kind of sundial—during the daytime, and a clock worked by the dripping of water during the hours of darkness. (Even today water clocks still exist; there is one in a hotel at Beaumaris in Anglesey.) Sundials were widely used during the Middle Ages. (See *Sundial*)

It was in this period of history that public clocks made their appearance, the first probably being that installed at Salisbury Cathedral in 1386. This instrument still exists and is one of the claimants to the title of the oldest clock in the world. It has no dial and was made to strike the hour only. There are other fourteenth-century clocks at Charterhouse in London and at Ottery St Mary, Exeter, Wells, and Wimborne. Those at the last three places were probably all made by the same man, Peter Lightfoot, a Glastonbury monk. It appears that only that at Ottery St Mary retains its original works. Another very old clock still using its original mechanism is in the church at Rye in Sussex; it is over four hundred years old and has a pendulum 24 feet long.

Until the seventeenth century many public clocks had no dials, because few people were able to read a dial. On many of these clocks the hours were sounded by mechanical figures called ' jacks '. (See *Clock Jack*.) A few dial-less timepieces survive; there is one at Appleby in Lincolnshire.

It was not until the seventeenth century, either, that the minute-hand mechanism was perfected, so that clocks made before that time often had only one hand. There are still more than twenty examples of this kind of timepiece, among them being the clocks at Coningsby in Lincolnshire and Northill in Bedfordshire.

There are several clocks which possess letters instead of figures on their dials. They can be seen at the following places (the words in brackets are the inscriptions formed by the dials): Baslow, Derbyshire (Victoria, 1897); West Acre, Norfolk (Watch and Pray); Buckland-on-the-Moor, Devon (My Dear Mother); Wootton Rivers, Wiltshire (Glory be to God).

Even rarer than clocks with letters instead of figures are six-sided time pieces. There are probably only two in the country: on a hotel in Brixton and at Clarence Dock in Liverpool. Liverpool also possesses the largest four-dial electric turret clock in England; it is in the Royal Liver Building and has dials 25 feet in diameter. It is interesting to learn that a method of controlling clocks by electricity was invented as long ago as 1842.

(See in this book the descriptions given under the following headings : *Act of Parliament Clock; Silent Clock; Water Clock*.)

Clock Jack. Clock dials did not come into use until the fourteenth century and consequently the only means of ascertaining the time from a clock was by its striking apparatus. Even for another two hundred years, clocks were often made without dials, for few people were capable of reading them.

The striking apparatus frequently consisted of an ingenious model of a human figure which struck a bell every quarter of an hour. This figure was known as a jack. One of the oldest of these, known as Jack Blandiver, is inside Wells Cathedral, which also has two other jacks on a clock on the exterior. Other Cathedrals with clock jacks are Norwich and York.

Cloud Pond. See *Dew Pond*

Cob Cottage. Cob is a mixture of clay and straw. There are many cob cottages in Devonshire. Usually they have a black band round the base; this is tar and its purpose is to keep out the wet.

Cock-pit. It is possible that the ancient Britons practised the cruel sport of cock-fighting, in which two birds were set to attack each other until one of them was killed. It seems unlikely, however, that special pits were constructed for cock-fights until Tudor times; Henry VIII had a pit constructed at Whitehall Palace. Cromwell banned the sport, but it became very popular again after the Restoration, when pits were built in many towns and villages.

These pits were usually about eighteen feet in diameter. Some of them were covered in; others were open. The floor was covered with turf or matting and the sides padded with hay and canvas. A few cock-pits still exist: there is one at a farm at Lydbury North in Shropshire, and a thatched cock-pit, scheduled as an ancient monument, stands in the yard of the Hawk and Buckle inn at Denbigh.

Cock-fighting maintained its popularity among both rich and poor throughout the Stuart and Georgian ages. Birds were bred specially for the sport and were given names, like race-horses. One of the most enthusiastic owners was the Earl of Derby, who founded the famous horse-race; he possessed three thousand fighting cocks and his wife is supposed to have divorced him because he insisted on holding cock-fights in the drawing-room.

In Victorian times a different view was taken of such sports and in 1849 Parliament passed an Act making it illegal to maintain public cock-pits. Private cock-fights were still permitted, however, and even in recent years secret fights have taken place, particularly in the north of England.

Sport in England, by Norman Wymer (Harrap, 1949)

Coffin Cover. Some churches retain a number of stones which were used as coffin covers or as sepulchral slabs. Most of them date from the twelfth and thirteenth centuries. Many of them have crosses carved upon them; on some there are also symbols indicating the trade of the deceased person. The later slabs often bear an effigy carved in low relief. The slabs were sometimes used as floor stones. There is a very fine collection of coffin covers at Bakewell in Derbyshire.

Coffin Table. See *Lych-gate*

Common. A common is land on which all the inhabitants of a parish or district are entitled to exercise certain rights. These rights usually consist of the entitlement to graze sheep and cattle, and may also include authority to dig turf or cut bracken for fuel. Because of these rights, the owner of the land—usually the lord of the manor—has been prevented from enclosing it or cultivating it.

Commons are really the waste land of the manors. Under the old manorial system, the poorest land was left waste, to be used by all the people in the parish. Because they had no manorial system, Scotland and Ireland have no commons. In England and Wales there are 2,000,000 acres of common lands, and 20,500 of these are within fifteen miles of Charing Cross.

In the eighteenth and early nineteenth centuries the desire to farm as much land as possible led to the passing of numerous Acts authorizing the enclosure of many commons. In more recent years there has been a reaction against enclosure and the Commons Preservation Act of 1876 made it a public nuisance to encroach on any common. The Ministry of Agriculture may authorize the enclosure of a common, but only if this can be shown to be beneficial to the people living in the district. The protection of common lands is one of the aims of the Commons, Open Spaces and Footpaths Preservation Society.

The law relating to common land is extremely complicated. There has been no survey of these lands since 1874. A Select Committee on Common Lands submitted a report to Parliament in 1913, but this did not lead to any legislation. Now a comprehensive review of the law is being carried out by a Royal Commission set up in 1955.

English Commons and Forests, by Lord Eversley (1894)
Common Lands and Inclosure, by E. C. Gonner (Macmillan, 1912)

Communal Bakehouse. See *Bakehouse*

Conservation Area. See *Nature Reserve*

Corpse Road. In the north of England there are some tracks which acquired the name of corpse roads, because it was along them that the dead of a village which lacked a burial ground were carried to the nearest village possessing a churchyard. Thus, until the middle of the fifteenth century, the dead of Eskdale in Cumberland had to be carried over Burnmoor to St Bees for burial. Another old corpse way can be followed from Keld to Grinton in Yorkshire.

Cortège Cross. See *Weeping Cross*

Courtyard House. Some of the settlements of the Iron Age (450 B.C.–A.D. 43) consisted of small numbers of stone-built houses, each of which was built around a courtyard. The walls of the house, which had several rooms, were sometimes 15 feet thick. Each house usually had an underground passage, which in Cornwall is known as a fogou (q.v.) and a terraced garden. The best preserved village of courtyard houses is at Chysauster in Cornwall.

Cresset. Some church towers had a large cylindrical copper vessel fixed to them. This vessel was known as a cresset and in it a fire was lit to signal the news of any important event, such as the coming of the Spanish Armada. The cresset on the tower of the church at Monken Hadley in Middlesex is believed to be the only one still in existence.

Cresset Stone. This is a flat stone with cup-shaped hollows in it in which oil or grease was placed. A wick was put in the oil or grease and lit to give illumination. This form of lighting was often used in churches. There is a cresset stone in Brecon Cathedral.

Cromlech. This is the name given by archaeologists to stone circles. It should not be used to describe circles of the embanked sanctuary type, like Stonehenge (see *Bronze Age Sanctuary*), but only those without external earthworks, like the Hurlers, at Linkinhorne in Cornwall. The Hurlers consist of three circles, but usually cromlechs are isolated. Sometimes the stones are placed on low banks, but normally the sites of the circles are level. Cromlechs are widely distributed over various parts of the country, from Cornwall in the south to Cumberland and Northumberland in the north. Although it is difficult to date them, most of them are believed to have been constructed in the Bronze Age. A number of them have legends associated with them which give a fanciful account of their erection.

Cross. The various types of crosses are described under the following headings:

> *Butter cross;*
> *Churchyard cross;*
> *Eleanor cross;*
> *High cross;*
> *Market cross;*
> *Memorial cross;*
> *Preaching cross;*
> *Sanctuary cross;*
> *Village cross;*
> *Wayside cross;*
> *Weeping cross.*

Cross-roads. The burial of suicides in churchyards used to be forbidden, and it was the practice to bury them at lonely cross-roads. The body was usually pierced with a spear or stake, which was pushed right through the body into the ground and was left there when the grave was filled in. This custom was supposed to prevent the suicide's spirit from haunting the locality. Despite this precaution, a number of cross-roads were supposed to be haunted.

Cup and Ring Carving. There are a variety of patterns in this type of Bronze Age carving, but the most common one is a circular hollow surrounded by incised rings. It is thought that the carving, which was made on rocks, had a religious significance. There are many of these markings on Rumbles Moor, Baildon Moor and Addington High Moor in Yorkshire. Some of the carvings have been brought from the moors and placed near Ilkley Church and there is also one in Keighley Museum.

Cursing Well. See *Well*

Cursus. This ancient monument consists of a long narrow strip of land between two banks. There is one of these strange earthworks—known as *the* Cursus—near Stonehenge. It is nearly two miles long and about 120 yards wide; it was named by an antiquarian who thought it might have been associated with ancient funeral celebrations. The name has been applied to similar monuments in the west and south of England, but most of them are visible only from the air.

D

Dam. A dam is a wall built across a valley in order to impound the water, so that it can be used to irrigate the land, to generate electricity, or for consumption by a community of people. Some dams also control the flow of water during seasons of heavy rainfall and thus help to prevent floods. The area of water impounded by a dam is known as a reservoir (q.v.).

There were dams in India and Ceylon as early as 500 B.C. They consisted of banks of earth, some of which were 70 feet high. The Romans built many dams of masonry.

Wales possesses some of the finest dams in Britain. The Vyrnwy Dam in Montgomeryshire, which is 1,172 feet long, was built in 1892 in order to form a reservoir to supply water to Liverpool, seventy miles away. There are several dams in the Elan valley, from which water is taken to Birmingham. The largest dam in the United Kingdom is the Claerwen Dam in Cardiganshire, which was opened in 1952. It is 1,166 feet long and its maximum height is 240 feet. The reservoir which it forms contains over ten thousand million gallons of water.

Date Panel. It has for long been the practice of builders to place a panel on houses bearing their initials and the date when the building was completed. Some panels have dates in the seventeenth century. The practice is still continued by some builders today, although it is not as common as it used to be. In some cases the builder included his wife's initials as well as his own.

Usually the panels are of stone, but in East Anglia, where stone is scarce, they are made of plaster. A variety of finely carved stone panels can be found in the Wirral district of Cheshire.

Deer-bone Floor. A floor made of deer-bones stuck in the ground, with the knuckle-end uppermost, is a rarity. There is a room with such a floor in the garden cottage of the National Trust garden at Killerton, near Exeter. An adjoining room has a log floor (q.v.). There is another deer-bone floor at Bicton, only a few miles from Killerton.

Deertrap. A large grating is sometimes placed in the ground at the entrance to a drive or at the gateway to a field. Animals find it impossible to walk over this grating, which is known as a deertrap, and so it prevents them from straying.

Dene Hole. In the chalk districts of southern England there are a number of artificial pits, known as dene holes. They are usually domed chambers about 16 feet high, approached by a circular shaft about 3 feet in diameter sunk vertically through the strata lying above the chalk. Sometimes the chamber is quite large and its roof is supported by chalk pillars.

Dene holes are usually grouped together. Most of them are in Kent and Essex; there are important groups at Grays Thurrock, Essex, and at Chislehurst, Kent.

The purpose for which they were made is a mystery, as is

the date of their construction. It has been suggested that they were storehouses or dwellings or merely workings for supplies of chalk. They appear to have been given their name because of a belief that they were either made by the Danes or were used by people fleeing from them.

Devil's Bridge. There are a number of bridges in Britain and on the continent which are supposed to have been constructed by the Devil. The story of the building of one of these, near Aberystwyth, tells how an old woman lost her cow and eventually found it but could not reach it because it was on the other side of a ravine. The Devil said he would bridge the ravine if the woman promised him the first living thing that crossed the bridge. She agreed, and the bridge was rapidly erected. Then the Devil beckoned to her to cross over and capture her cow, but she was more cunning than he had thought, for she called her dog and sent him after a crust of bread which she threw across. So the only reward the Devil received was the old woman's dog.

Similar tales are told of the other Devil's Bridges. One of these is at Kirkby Lonsdale in Westmorland.

Dew Pond. On the chalk hills of southern England there are pools known as dew ponds. These are artificial ponds, and they are remarkable because, although they are far from springs or streams, they seldom dry up.

At one time dew-pond makers travelled from farm to farm, making new ponds and repairing old ones, but now the craft has died out. Their first step in constructing a new pond was to cut a saucer-shaped hollow in the ground, between four and six feet deep at the centre. The bottom of this hollow was covered with clay, on which was placed a layer of dry straw. Then broken chalk or rubble was used to cover the straw, and water was poured into the hollow. Once water was placed in it, the pond would remain filled.

For centuries the principle on which the dew pond worked was something of a mystery. It seems quite simple, however. The straw is a non-conductor of heat, and therefore the base of the pond remains cool. When darkness falls the cool clay attracts more moisture from the atmosphere than does the earth surrounding it. Experiments have shown that very little of this moisture is dew; by far the greater quantity comes from mists.

The method of making dew ponds appears to date from ancient times. Such ponds would seem to be the obvious source of a water supply for people dwelling in prehistoric camps, which were usually placed on hilltops.

Dewponds are also known as mist ponds, cloud ponds, fog ponds, and sheep ponds.

Disk Barrow. See *Round Barrow*

Dog Gate. This fixture is still to be found in a few old country houses, usually at the foot of the staircase. It is a relic of the days when hounds roamed the ground floors of the great houses, but were prevented by such gates from reaching the bedrooms.

Dog Tongs. Dogs often used to follow their owners to church and stray dogs sometimes wandered into church during the service. In many country districts there was often a man to whom was allotted the task of expelling dogs which became disorderly. To enable him to do this with as little disturbance as possible he was provided with a whip and some tongs, which he used to grip the dog's neck. Some of these tongs are preserved, chiefly in churches in Wales and Scotland. There is a pair at Clynnog Fawr, in Caernarvonshire.

Dog-whipper's Bench. In some churches it used to be the task of one or two men to drive intruding dogs from the church with whips. Benches were provided for these men near the door. The church at Ormskirk in Lancashire still possesses its dog-whippers' benches, and a whip is preserved at Baslow in Derbyshire.

Dole Cupboard. In some towns and villages money was bequeathed by local benefactors to provide bread for the poorer inhabitants. The bread was usually distributed at the church on Sundays, and in order to obtain it the poor people had to attend the service. Often there was a cupboard in the church which was set aside for the storage of the bread; this was known as a dole cupboard. There is one of these cupboards at West Chiltington in Sussex. Sometimes a rack was used instead of a cupboard. (See *Bread Rack*)

Dole Table. In some churchyards, such as that at Norton Malreward in Somerset, there is a large flat stone from which the money belonging to various charities was distributed. Occasionally the tombstone of the benefactor was used for this purpose.

Dolmen. A dolmen is a New Stone Age burial chamber, consisting of two or more upright stones with a flat stone placed on top of them as a roof. The bodies were placed within the chamber thus formed and the whole structure was then covered with a mound of earth. A well-known dolmen is Kit's Coty House, near Aylesford, Kent; the roof stone of this weighs ten tons. Dolmens are commonest, however, in Cornwall and Wales. They are sometimes referred to as cromlechs, but this name should really only be used for certain types of stone circles. (See *Cromlech*)

Donkey Wheel. See *Tread Wheel*

Dovecote. Until the practice of growing root crops was adopted, large numbers of cattle had to be slaughtered at the commencement of each winter because of the lack of feeding stuffs for them. This meant, of course, that there was no fresh meat during the winter, and as a step towards overcoming this difficulty pigeons were kept. To house these birds, dovecotes were erected, although originally only the lord of the manor and the priest were allowed to build these structures.

Today several hundred of them remain, mostly dating from the sixteenth and seventeenth centuries. One of the oldest dovecotes is at Patcham in Sussex; it was built six hundred years ago and could accommodate 550 birds. It is circular, but in later times rectangular dovecotes become more common.

Some dovecotes were fitted with a device called a potence, which consisted of a ladder fixed to a revolving frame to enable all the nests to be reached without difficulty.

In Wales dovecotes are rare. One of the few specimens is at Penmon in Anglesey.

Ducking Stool. Ducking stools were instruments used in the punishment of quarrelsome married folk, dishonest tradesmen, and women who were scolds. Although sometimes men were punished by ducking, it was usually women who were made to suffer in this way, while male offenders were placed in the pillory or the stocks.

The ducking stool consisted of a chair attached to a long beam, which was pivoted to a post at the edge of the village pond. The victim was tied in the chair which was then moved into the pond by means of the beam. Sometimes the stool was fitted with wheels so that the unfortunate occupant could be dragged through the village before being ducked.

Ducking stools were probably first employed as a means of punishment in the fifteenth century. A stool which is preserved at Leominster was used in 1817, although on that occasion the sentence could not be properly carried out because there was no water in the pond at the time. There is no record of a stool being used after that date.

Dumb Borsholder. This is a symbol of authority used originally in Saxon times. It consisted of an oaken staff fitted with a ring and an iron point. The keeper of this staff, who was elected annually, was entitled to collect certain rates. For example, the holder of the dumb borsholder in the church at Wateringbury in Kent collected a penny from every house in a nearby hamlet. Dumb borsholders are now extremely rare; that at Wateringbury may be the only one in existence. Until 1748 it was formally presented every year at the Court Leet of the Hundred.

Dyke. This is the name given by archaeologists to long banks or ditches. These banks and ditches were first made by the Belgae, a tribe who invaded Britain in the last fifty years B.C., but the two best-known dykes are of much later date. Wansdyke, which begins near Inkpen in Berkshire and runs fifty miles westward to the Somerset coast, was probably not completed until the second half of the fifth century A.D. Offa's Dyke, which stretches for a hundred and thirty miles from Chepstow to Prestatyn, was not built until the eighth century.

Dykes were seldom erected for defensive purposes, but usually to mark a boundary. Offa's Dyke served to separate the Saxon kingdom of Mercia from Wales.

A Guide to the Prehistoric and Roman Monuments of England and Wales, by Jacquetta Hawkes (Chatto and Windus, 1951)

E

Eleanor Cross. Eleanor Crosses mark the places at which the body of Eleanor of Castile, queen of Edward I, rested on the journey from Harby, Notts, where she died, to Westminster Abbey. It is thought that at least ten of these crosses were erected, but only three remain—at Geddington and Hardingstone in Northants and at Waltham in Essex. London's Charing Cross replaces one of the original Eleanor Crosses.

Embanked Sanctuary. See *Bronze Age Sanctuary*

Enclosure. This name is used on Ordnance Survey maps for earthworks about which little is known. They do not appear to have been used for military purposes and the date of their construction is uncertain. It is assumed that they were enclosures for animals. There are large numbers of them in Pembrokeshire, Carmarthenshire, and the Scottish Lowlands.

F

Family and Commercial Hotel. Many old inns bear this description on their walls. It is a practice which dates from about 1840, when middle-class families first started going on holidays.

Fingerpost. See *Signpost*

Fire Hook. Long hooks used to be available in many villages to draw burning thatch from roofs when fires occurred. There are a few places where these hooks are still kept in the church; Iver, Bucks, is one of them.

Firemark. At one time the only fire brigades in the country were those employed by the various insurance companies. These brigades would fight fires only if the property was insured with their company; there are instances on record of firemen arriving at the scene of a fire and, on finding that the owner was not so insured, standing idly by while the house burned down. Consequently it was necessary to have some indication that a building was insured with a particular company. This was the purpose of firemarks, which were metal plates, fixed to the walls of houses, bearing the company's badge and often the number of the insurance policy.

Many of these firemarks, most of which were erected between two hundred and three hundred years ago, can still be seen today. The earliest ones were made of lead; later marks were of copper or iron. A very common one is that of the Sun Fire Office. One less frequently found is that of the Protector Insurance Company, showing a fireman fighting the flames.

Some very cautious people insured their property with several different companies so that their houses were decorated with a number of firemarks. Such a collection is to be seen on some cottages at Sutton Courtenay in Berkshire.

An inn sign, Partridge Green, Sussex

Oratory, subsequently a lock-up, on the bridge at Bradford-on-Avon, Wiltshire

Coffin table, Chiddingfold, Surrey

Fives Court. The game of fives developed during the Middle Ages and consisted originally of using one's hands to knock a ball against a wall. The churchyard wall was found to be very convenient for this purpose and sometimes a part of the churchyard was hollowed out especially to form a fives court. There is a depression in the ground near the church at Craswall in Dorset which may have served this purpose. It is interesting to note that the game of Eton fives originated with the schoolboys playing against the wall of the chapel.

Flint Mine. This is a pit from which New Stone Age men obtained the flints which they fashioned into weapons. Flint mines are found only in chalk country, since it was there that shafts could be sunk to reach the beds of flint some distance below the surface. These shafts, some of which had side-galleries radiating from them, were dug with antlers, which the men who did the quarrying used as picks. The most interesting flint mines are at Grimes Graves, near Brandon in Suffolk, an area where flint-knapping is still carried on. Another important flint-mining centre was on Cissbury Ring, near Worthing in Sussex, where the mounds and depressions of the filled in mines can be seen.

Fog Pond. See *Dew Pond*

Fogou. This is the name given by the Cornish people to the underground passages which were apparently used as places of refuge by the inhabitants of courtyard houses (q.v.) and some of the Iron Age forts. The finest fogou is at Halligye near Trelowarren, where the passages were formed by digging deep trenches, lining them with drystone walling, and roofing them with large slabs.

Folk Museum. The aim of a folk museum is to show the way in which the people of a country lived in the past—the way they worked and the manner in which they spent their leisure. Britain was slow in developing this type of museum, which is well-known in the Scandinavian countries. The Welsh Folk Museum was opened at St Fagan's Castle near Cardiff in 1946. It has rooms completely equipped with furniture of certain

D

periods. The Museum also endeavours to show how certain trades were carried on; thus a wood-turner and a basket-maker can be seen at work.

Three years after the opening of St Fagan's, Bristol's folk museum was established at Blaise Castle House. Besides possessing within its rooms a good collection of furniture and agricultural implements it has in its grounds an eighteenth-century water mill, which was moved from a Somerset village and re-erected.

Folly. Scattered over the countryside are a number of buildings known as follies, but it is difficult to define exactly what is meant by this word. Usually a folly was erected to serve no utilitarian purpose, although there are some exceptions to this. Many follies date from the eighteenth and early nineteenth centuries; their builders thought their work improved the landscape. Some were in the form of sham castles; a well-known one is that erected near Bath by Ralph Allen in 1762. No expense was spared in the erection of these follies; Racton Tower, a sham ruin in Sussex, cost £10,000 when it was erected by Lord Halifax in 1770.

The tower was the most common type of folly. Usually they were erected either as ruins, like that at Racton, or in order to obtain a better view over the surrounding country-side—Beckford's Folly near Bath is an example of this. Some-times they were built as memorials, like the tower at Drysllwyn in Carmarthenshire, which commemorates the achievements of Nelson.

Some men had a mania for constructing follies; not content with one, they erected several. Mad Jack Fuller, a Member of Parliament who died in 1834, was responsible for no less than six at Dallington and Brightling in Sussex. They include his own tombstone, a huge pyramid in Brightling churchyard.

The newest folly appears to be that at Faringdon in Berkshire which was erected in 1935 by the fourteenth Lord Berners. It is a tower 140 feet high, designed by the Duke of Wellington.

Follies and Grottoes, by Barbara Jones (Constable, 1953)

Footpath. The short cut afforded by a footpath was once a much-used feature of the countryside. Unfortunately the great increase in the number of people travelling by mechanical means of transport has led to a decline in the use of footpaths and the consequent disappearance of many of them. Others were lost during the last war, when they were ploughed up in the farmers' great effort to provide more food. There is, however, a movement to preserve the remaining footpaths, which provide a means of travelling that is pleasant and peaceful when compared with the noise of the roads. Two bodies have both played important parts in this movement: they are the Commons, Open Spaces and Footpaths Preservation Society and the Ramblers' Association.

Ford. The oldest type of river crossing is the ford, and many of our towns and villages grew up at points where streams could be forded. This is shown by the large number of them which incorporate the word *ford* in their names.

Although the Romans constructed bridges to carry many of their roads over rivers they used fords extensively. In their days some of the rivers which are now quite deep were much shallower. It is possible that they were able to ford the Thames at London, and Lord Noel-Buxton has endeavoured to prove that they forded the estuaries of the Humber and the Severn by walking across them himself in 1953 and 1954.

The fords were often marked with stakes. Some of them were paved by constructing a stone causeway beneath the water. This was done so that carts and chariots should not get stuck in the mud. There is an example of a paved ford near Evesham.

There are still a few fords in use, but in many cases bridges have been constructed beside them.

Former Ports. There are a number of places around the coast that were once thriving ports, but which have lost their prosperity and trade and are now only small villages. Usually this has been brought about because of changing tides or receding seas.

The Dee estuary provides several examples of ports ruined by receding seas. In Roman and Saxon times Chester was a port, but in the Middle Ages ships could no longer reach there, so they went to Shotwick instead. In the fourteenth century Shotwick was replaced by Burton, which in its turn gave way to Parkgate, where the sands are now turned into marshland, although some of the harbour works can still be seen. When Parkgate could no longer be used, an attempt was made to construct a harbour at Dawpool, but the work had to be abandoned because of the silting of the river.

The first cotton imported into Britain came to a forgotten port. This was Sunderland, on the Lancashire coast.

Other places which were once prosperous ports include Blakeney and Cley in Norfolk, Dunwich in Suffolk, Seaford in Sussex, and Portmadoc in Carnarvonshire.

Fort. See *Hill-fort*

Fortified Bridge. See *War Bridge*

Fortified Vicarage. When England and Scotland were often at war with each other and border raids between the two countries were frequent, some vicarages in Northumberland were built as fortresses. When warning was received of the approach of the Scots, all the villagers hastened to the vicarage and stayed there until the raid was over. There is a fortified vicarage at Embleton.

Fountain. There were fountains in ancient Babylon nearly five thousand years ago, and they were very common in ancient Greece.

In this country they were usually erected only on the estates of wealthy people until the nineteenth century, when many towns provided simple drinking fountains for horses and sometimes for human beings as well. The Metropolitan Drinking Fountain Association was formed in 1859.

In a street in Bath there is a drinking fountain supplied by warm water. This comes from the city's famous hot springs.

French Buttress. This type of buttress, consisting of a pillar supporting a wall, is very rare in England. It is likely that the French buttresses beside the wall of the Old Monastery Garden at Edington in Wiltshire are the only ones in the country.

Frid Stool, or Frith Stool. From Saxon times until the reign of James I wrongdoers fleeing from justice could claim sanctuary in churches or monasteries. The right of sanctuary often commenced in the courtyard and extended to the altar, and the penalty for violating this right increased as the high altar or the frith stool was approached. This frith stool was a chair for the fugitive placed near the altar. Today only two of them remain—at Hexham Abbey in Northumberland and at Beverley Minster in Yorkshire. There are also seats in Chewton Mendip church, Somerset, and in Halsham church, Yorkshire, which it is thought were probably used for the same purpose. The violation of the frith stool at Beverley was considered so grave an offence that it was punishable by death.

Funeral Garland. In some villages it used to be the custom to carry garlands made of white paper at the funeral of unmarried women. Paper gloves were usually attached to the garlands to symbolize a challenge to anybody who might doubt the purity of the deceased person. After the funeral the garlands were hung in the church, and there are a few places where they are still preserved. They include Matlock in Derbyshire and Abbotts Ann in Hampshire. At the latter village the garlands were formed into a crown, known as the virgin's crown.

Abbotts Ann is the only place where the custom of carrying funeral garlands still survives. It was revived in 1953 after a lapse of more than thirty years. Some of the garlands hanging in the church are more than two centuries old. The custom at Abbotts Ann is unique in another respect, for it was observed not only at the funerals of unmarried women but also at the burials of youths.

Furnace Pond, or **Hammer Pond.** In the sixteenth century the iron smelting industry was not concentrated in the Midlands but in Kent, Sussex, and Surrey. These counties possessed both iron ore and the fuel used to smelt it, which was not coal but wood converted into charcoal. So much timber was used for this purpose that the forests began to disappear rapidly, so that the governments of the time introduced measures aimed at limiting the devastation.

A relic of this iron industry is the furnace pond or hammer pond. A stream was dammed to form a pond and the fall of water at the lower end was used to work the bellows which provided the blast for the furnaces and also to turn a wheel which operated a hammer for beating the iron into sheets. A number of these ponds remain, although all other signs of the activity which went on around them have disappeared, except, perhaps, for some iron tombstones in the churchyard or local names of woods or fields which incorporate the words *furnace* or *forge*. One Surrey village, Abinger Hammer, takes its name from the ponds there.

G

Gad Whip. This is a relic of a curious custom by which a piece of land was held as long as the tenant came to church on a certain Sunday each year and cracked a whip during the service. A gad whip is preserved in the church at Caistor in Lincolnshire. There the tenant concerned had to attend the church on Palm Sunday, crack the whip during the reading of the first lesson, and then kneel down and wave the whip three times over the parson's head while the second lesson was being read. He then had to place the whip, together with a purse containing thirty silver pennies and three pieces of wych elm, in a certain pew. This custom was last carried out in 1846.

Gallows. See *Gibbet*

Gate. There are so many types of gates that it is not possible to describe them all in this book. The commonest on farmland is undoubtedly the five-barred gate, but in different parts of the country there are varying ways of arranging the upright and diagonal bars on this.

In the north of England the gates often have four or five

uprights and a diagonal which stretches right across the gate, but in the southern counties there are usually only two uprights and the diagonal bar extends across only part of the gate. In Hampshire the uprights are evenly spaced, but in Wiltshire they are often placed closer together at one end of the gate. Warwickshire also has its uprights close together, but instead of only one diagonal there are two.

In sheep-farming districts gates with only two crossbars are sometimes seen. These gates are used for counting sheep. The space between the bottom bar and the ground is fairly large, but not big enough to admit a sheep unless its head is pressed down slightly. The shepherd who wishes to count his flock or to separate certain sheep from the others gets all the flock on one side of the gate and then takes each sheep in turn, presses its head down and pushes it under the bottom bar. This simple method is usually quite effective because the sheep seem quite unwilling to take the trouble to lower their heads and pass under the gate without being forced to do so.

A kissing gate is one which can be used only by pedestrians. It swings within an angular or circular cage so that only one person can pass through at a time. The object of this design is to permit the passage of human beings while preventing that of animals. It acquired its name because youths sometimes demanded a kiss from the village girls before allowing them to pass through the gate.

A peculiar type is the tumble or clapper gate, the top bar of which has to be pressed in order that the walker can pass through. When he reaches the other side and relaxes the pressure, weights which hang at the end of the bars restore them to their original position. There is one of these gates at the entrance to the churchyard at Hungerford, Berkshire.

Gate-house. A gate-house is the name given to a dwelling built over the gateway at the entrance to a large estate. Gate-houses were erected not only on the property of wealthy noblemen, but also on ecclesiastical estates. Worksop in Nottinghamshire still has its priory gate-house. There is a fine timbered gate-house to a privately owned estate at Crowhurst in Surrey.

Gibbet. This word is sometimes used to indicate a gallows on which criminals were hanged, but normally it is the name given to a post with a projecting arm at the top on which the body of a person was hung in chains after he had been executed elsewhere. This practice was supposed to serve as a warning to other malefactors. It was not part of the legal sentence and was not recognized by law until 1752. It was abolished in 1834.

None of the original gibbets remain, for they were usually placed on exposed sites and consequently they have succumbed to the weather. In several cases, however, their positions are marked by reproductions, as at Ditchling Common in Sussex, Steng Cross in Northumberland, and on Inkpen Beacon in Berkshire.

The gibbet on Ditchling Common is known as Jacob's Post because the body of a pedlar named Jacob Harris was suspended from it in 1734. He had been hanged at Horsham after being found guilty of murdering three people. The people of Ditchling and the surrounding district used to believe that if they carried a piece of Jacob's Post around with them they would be protected from toothache.

The Inkpen gibbet has to be kept in repair by the tenant of a nearby farm; this is one of the conditions attached to the lease of the farm. The original gibbet was set up in 1676 to bear the bodies of George Bromman and Dorothy Newman, who had been convicted of the murder of Bromman's wife.

Gossip's Bridle, Scold's Bridle, or **Brank.** This curious instrument of punishment consisted of two iron rings which fitted over a woman's head and a bit which was fastened in her mouth, to prevent her from gossiping or scolding. There is a gossip's bridle in the church at Walton-on-Thames, Surrey.

Green Road. See *Ancient Trackway*

Grotto. In the eighteenth century many wealthy persons thought it fashionable to construct artificial caverns in the grounds of their mansions and decorate them with shells.

There is a famous grotto at Twickenham which was made by Alexander Pope about 1720. Other grottoes include that in Goodwood Park, Sussex, constructed by the second Duchess of Richmond, and that at Clifton, Bristol, which was the work of Thomas Goldeney. This grotto took nearly thirty years to complete.

Follies and Grottoes, by Barbara Jones (Constable, 1953)

Guildhall. Guildhalls were originally the meeting-places of the medieval associations of merchants and craftsmen. These powerful bodies gradually obtained control of local government, and although the guilds disappeared centuries ago, their guildhalls are often still used as municipal or county halls. The best-known guildhall is, of course, that of the City of London, but there are many others of historical interest. York's fifteenth-century guildhall was badly damaged in an air raid. Lavenham in Sussex has a beautiful half-timbered guildhall; that at Hereford, known as The Old House, is also half-timbered.

H

Ha-ha. This strange name is given to a ditch constructed to form a boundary to a garden or park without interrupting the view. It was often unnoticeable to anybody approaching it until he had almost fallen into it, and the name is supposed to be derived from the exclamation of surprise. There is a ha-ha in the Old Deer Park at Richmond in Surrey which is supposed to have been made by George III, who kept sheep in the park.

Hammer Pond. See *Furnace Pond*

Healing Well. See *Well*

Hermitage. The strange passion of the eighteenth and early nineteenth centuries for constructing follies and grottoes was accompanied by a mania for building hermitages, where some man would dwell all alone for many years. Men actually earned their living by being hermits and advertisements for them are to be found in the newspapers of the time. There is a good example of a hermitage at Burley on the Hill in Rutland.

Follies and Grottoes, by Barbara Jones (Constable, 1953)

High Cross. The fine sculptured crosses erected by the Saxons are often called high crosses. The earliest ones date from the seventh century and are to be found in the Scottish border country; there is one at Ruthwell in Dumfries and another at Bewcastle. The vogue of constructing these crosses gradually spread southwards and reached South Wales in the ninth or tenth century. There is a richly ornamented cross at Carew in Pembrokeshire. High crosses are sometimes known as Anglian crosses, apparently from the belief that they were made by the Angles.

Hill Figure, or **Hillside Figure.** These seem to be the commonest names for those massive pictures cut in various parts of the chalk downlands, although they are also known as chalk figures and turf cuttings.

England appears to have more of these figures than any other country, and nearly all of them are in the south. By far the commonest type is the white horse, which is described separately in this book.

When the inhabitants of this country first started to use the downland as a canvas is unknown. The oldest hill figure, the white horse at Uffington in Berkshire, is thought to date from the Early Iron Age.

Another mystery is the reason that prompted the construction of these figures. It is well known that many of the more modern ones were commemorative, but the earlier figures were not mentioned in written records until they were already centuries old. In the case of the older cuttings, it seems more likely that religious beliefs led to their construction.

Most of the figures are solid white cuttings, but a few are in outline only. The latter include the famous giant at Cerne Abbas in Dorset and the Long Man at Wilmington in Sussex.

The Cerne giant is probably the second oldest of the hill figures. It may have been cut in the second century A.D., possibly as a symbol of fertility. Wilmington's Long Man is larger than Cerne's giant—its height of 240 feet makes it the biggest representation of the human figure in the world. Various theories have been put forward as to the date of its construction and it has been suggested that both figures were made by monks —there were monasteries at Cerne and at Wilmington.

In addition to the horses and the giants, there are a number of other hill figures. They include a stag at Mormond in Aberdeenshire, white crosses at Whiteleaf and Bledlow in the Chilterns, a number of regimental badges at Fovant in Wiltshire, and a lion near Whipsnade Zoo. This lion appears to be the most recently constructed figure; it was cut in 1933.

From time to time all the chalk figures have to be cleaned, otherwise they become overgrown with turf. This is a lengthy and somewhat costly business, and unfortunately a number of hill figures have completely disappeared because nobody took the trouble to maintain them.

White Horses and Other Hill Figures, by Morris Marples
    (Country Life, 1949)

Hill-fort. Forts, usually found on hill-tops, are a common form of prehistoric remains. They are particularly abundant on the chalk downs of southern England. There are various types, most of which date from the Iron Age (450 B.C.–A.D. 43). The sites can be recognized by the ramparts, which usually follow the contours of the hill-top.

Often these forts are in fine situations, and the climb to them is well worth while because of the view which is obtained, even though there may now be little trace of the fort itself. Two examples of forts which are excellent viewpoints are those on the Wrekin in Shropshire and on the Breiddin in Montgomeryshire.

Besides the forts of the chalk downs there are others in the stone country of the north of England. The sites of these are marked by the remains of overgrown stone walls, such as those on Yeavering Bell in Northumberland.

Today all that remains of many downland forts is a bank and a ditch, but when they were originally constructed they were far more impressive. The Iron Age forts can be divided into three parts. The earliest and simplest usually have only a single rampart which follows the contour of the hill. The construction of these ramparts entailed a considerable amount of work. Sixty thousand tons of earth were dug to form that of the camp on Cissbury Hill, near Worthing, and it was protected by a wall of timber. At the entrance to the fort there were wooden gates.

Maiden Castle, near Dorchester, the best-known of all the Iron Age camps, belongs to the second type. These had complex defences: Maiden Castle has seven lines of bank and fosse, and some of its ramparts are 50 feet high.

Camps of the third type are comparatively few in number. They are those which were constructed by a tribe known as the Belgae. Examples are to be seen at Oldbury near Ightham in Kent and at Hod Hill in Dorset. It is often difficult to distinguish the camps of the Belgae, for often they adapted existing camps to their own use. The most prominent features of their camps are usually very deep, wide boundary ditches.

Most of the forts of the Early Iron Age appear to have been used only as places where the local population could take refuge temporarily when an attack by invaders seemed imminent, but there are a few which seem to have been inhabited for fairly long periods.

Britain B.C., by S. E. Winbolt (Penguin Books, 1943)
A Guide to the Prehistoric and Roman Monuments in England and Wales, by Jacquetta Hawkes (Chatto and Windus, 1951)

Hog-backed Stone. This type of Saxon monument is found only in the north of England. It consists of a recumbent stone whose upper surface is rounded and carved with symbols. There are a number of hog-backed stones at Heysham in Lancashire.

Horse-drawn Tramway. As electric trams have almost disappeared from our streets it is strange to find that there is still one horse-drawn tramway. It is in the Isle of Man and operates only during the summer months.

Hour-glass Stand. Before watches came into use, clergymen frequently timed their sermons by means of an hour-glass, and often a metal stand for the hour-glass was fitted to the pulpit or in a convenient position nearby. Over a hundred of these stands can be found in English churches, and a few of them, like that at Warnham in Sussex, still have their hour-glasses.

House of Correction. See *Lock-up*

Housed Bridge. See *Bridge*

Hut Circle. This is the name given to the stone foundation walls of the huts used by prehistoric people. The huts, which were circular, were roofed with branches and turf. At the entrance there was a pair of large jamb-stones, and these usually form the most conspicuous feature of the circle today. The circles vary in diameter from 6 feet to 30 feet. Sometimes a low stone wall was built around a group of huts; on Dartmoor, where about thirteen hundred hut circles remain, this wall is known as a pound.

A Guide to the Prehistoric and Roman Monuments in England and Wales, by Jacquetta Hawkes (Chatto and Windus, 1951)

Hutment. See *Beehive Hut*

I

Ice-house, or **Ice-pit.** In olden days the owners of great houses often made their servants collect ice in the winter and bury it in a pit for use in the summer. The pit was kept cool by covering it with a mound of earth and planting trees on and around

the mound. A few of these pits still remain; there are several in Kent and there is another at Croome Court in Worcestershire.
Inn. This very well-known feature of the countryside really dates from the fourteenth century. There were certainly inns long before that date, even as far back as Roman times, but they were found only in the larger towns, while here and there along the highways were a few alehouses and taverns. In villages where there was an especial need for accommodation for travellers, this was usually provided by the Church, for often the travellers were pilgrims. Glastonbury, in Somerset, possesses one of these inns—it was, in fact, at one time known as The Pilgrim's Inn, but now it is The George Hotel. Only the wealthier travellers could afford to stay at such places, but there were often outbuildings where very rough accommodation was provided for poorer wayfarers.

With the decline of the monasteries and the decrease in the power of the church, the inn began to play an important part in social life. Another factor also helped the inn to become a national institution: this was the increase in commerce, and particularly the growth of the wool trade, which made it necessary for merchants to travel widely.

Inns were now built at places where these travellers were likely to stop for the night—at villages and at the junctions of the highways, as well as in towns. The fifteenth century saw the establishment of larger inns, like The Angel at Grantham and The George at Norton St Philip in Somerset. The peaceful years of the next century brought an even greater increase in the number of inns, for people began to travel for pleasure as well as for business. The licensing system, with rules for the conduct of inns, began in 1550. By 1577 there were nearly nine hundred alehouses, inns, and taverns in the county of Middlesex. Some fine Elizabethan inns remain—The Feathers at Ludlow is a well-known example. These inns were usually built in quadrangular form, around a courtyard, which was reached through a large gateway in the front of the building.

The establishment of stage coach services about the middle

of the seventeenth century gave a further impetus to the growth of the inn. The White Hart at Scole in Norfolk is typical of the inns erected at that time. Improvements both to roads and to vehicles in the eighteenth century led to another increase in travelling.

During the past four hundred years there had been changes in the service provided at the inns, as well as in the buildings themselves. The vermin-infested dormitories in which travellers had to sleep in the fourteenth century had gradually given place to clean, well-furnished bedrooms. There had been vast improvements, too, in the food provided.

The Victorian era saw the building of ugly hotels and gin-palaces. For this the growth of industrialism and the railways was largely to blame. The present century, with its many motorists, has, however, brought prosperity again to the older and better type of inn.

The Old Inns of England, by A. E. Richardson (Batsford, 1934)
The British Inn, by Thomas Burke (Longmans, Green, 1931)

Inn Sign. The Romans placed signs over their various commercial establishments. Their sign for a tavern was a bush; they used a real bush and not a painting.

In England in the Middle Ages, when few people could read, many tradesmen erected signs over their shops. The use of signs in this way was quite optional, except in the case of innkeepers; in 1393 a law was passed compelling the London publicans to place signs outside their taverns. It may be due to this compulsion that the custom of displaying signs outside public houses never died out.

The study of inn signs is a fascinating subject, largely because of the extraordinary number of different signs in use. All manner of objects—human, animal, vegetable, and mineral——are portrayed on the signboards.

A large class of signs show heraldic arms. It is thought that innkeepers adopted the arms of local noble families, hoping thus to persuade travellers that they enjoyed the patronage of these families. Some signs present strange combinations of objects, like The Bell and Mackerel or The Lion and Fiddle. Many of these were probably the result of two innkeepers entering into partnership and combining the names of their taverns.

Another group of strange signs arose from the corruption of certain phrases. Thus The Bull and Mouth was originally The Boulogne Mouth—Boulogne Harbour, the scene of a minor English victory in Tudor times.

Many signs portray famous people, although some of these personages are now almost forgotten. Few people who see General Abercromby's portrait on an inn sign in Arundel know that he was one of our leading soldiers at the end of the eighteenth century. Important events are also commemorated; the most commonly celebrated of these is probably the escape of Charles II after the Battle of Worcester, which is recalled by the numerous Royal Oaks.

In the late eighteenth and early nineteenth centuries the manufacture of inn signs was quite an industry, its main centre being in Harp Alley, off Shoe Lane in London. Often well-known artists were employed to paint signs. In the latter part of the nineteenth and early part of the twentieth centuries there was little enthusiasm for inn signs, but in the past twenty or thirty years there has been a great revival of interest. In 1936 a very successful exhibition of inn signs was held in London. The opening of a number of new inns since the end of the second world war has given artists the opportunity to create some original designs.

English Inn Signs, being a revised and modernized version of ' History of Signboards ', by Jacob Larwood and John Camden Hotten (Chatto and Windus, 1951)

Quaint Signs of Olde Inns, by C. J. Monson-Fitzjohn (Herbert Jenkins, 1926)

Inn-Signs—Their History and Meaning, by Sir Gurney Benham (The Brewers' Society, 1939)

Inn-Signia (The Whitbread Library, 1948)

Mass dial, March Baldon, Oxfordshire

A ' Bow Bells ' milestone

Iron Age Fort. See *Hill-fort*

Iron Mine. There are now few remains of mines from which the men of the Iron Age and the Romans obtained their iron, but at Lydney in Gloucestershire there is the shaft of a Roman mine.

Iron Ring. When the normal means of travel was on horseback, a small iron ring was often fixed to the wall near the entrance to inns or farms. The horse's reins were fastened through this, thus tethering the horse while its owner was conducting his business at the farm or refreshing himself at the inn. These rings are also to be found near some private houses.

J

Joanna House. See *Ash House*

K

Kissing Gate. See *Gate*

Kist or **Kistvaen** is the name given to a small kind of dolmen (q.v.).

L

Lewis Hole. Before cranes and similar lifting devices were invented, blocks of building stone were raised by means of an appliance called a lewis. This appliance was fitted into holes

E

cut in the stone. Lewis holes can be seen in the walls of the seventh-century church of St Peter-ad-Murum at Bradwell-on-Sea in Essex.

Library. See *Public Library*

Lich-gate. See *Lych-gate*

Lifeboat House. Lifeboats are generally kept in houses on the shore. Usually a lifeboat house has a slipway down which the lifeboat slides when it is launched and most of them are provided with winches for hauling up the boats. Reinforced concrete is the material most commonly used in the construction of slipways. The longest slipway (351 feet) is at Porthdinllaen in Caernarvonshire. The former lifeboat house at Port Eynon in Glamorganshire has been converted into a youth hostel.

Lighthouse. In ancient times towers with beacon fires were erected to guide mariners and warn them of dangerous rocks. The seven wonders of the world included a lighthouse, the Pharos of Alexandria, which was built in the reign of Ptolemy II (283–247 B.C.). It was a tower of white marble and is supposed to have been 600 feet high.

The earliest lighthouse in England was built by the Romans at Dover. It was probably about 80 feet high; the 40-foot tower which still remains was partly rebuilt in medieval times. The Romans are also believed to have erected lighthouses at Flamborough Head and at Holywell.

Prior to the reign of Henry VIII coast lighting was usually carried out by monks or priests. Often lights were placed in the towers of churches near the coast. Sometimes monks built towers solely for the purpose of holding warning lights; one of these towers still stands on Chale Down in the Isle of Wight. There used to be an oratory adjoining it in which a priest lived; it was his task to ensure that the light burned all night and to say mass for those who were lost at sea. During the seventeenth and eighteenth centuries many towers with braziers were built along the coasts.

Today there are over six hundred major and one thousand minor lights around the shores of the British Isles. Those in

England are administered by Trinity House and those in Scotland by the Commissioners of Northern Lights, while Irish light-houses are controlled by the Commissioners of Irish Lights. The cost of maintenance is derived from tolls on shipping known as 'light dues'.

Coal fire beacons were used to supply the light until 1822. In the eighteen-seventies oil gas was introduced, while electricity, which is now the usual source of light, was first used in 1858.

Some of the lighthouses are open to the public at certain times. They include the brightest lighthouse in England, that at St Catherine's in the Isle of Wight. The tallest lighthouse in the United Kingdom is on Bishop Rock in the Scilly Isles; it is 146 feet high.

British Lighthouses, by J. S. Wryde (1913)
The Romance of Lighthouses, by J. W. Corbin (Seeley Service, 1926)

Limekiln. Many estates used to have limekilns in which lime was burnt for agricultural purposes. The ruins of these can sometimes be seen. In some places the former presence of a kiln is indicated by the inclusion of the words 'limekiln' or 'kiln' in the name of a field or a house.

Link Extinguisher. In towns such as Bath in the eighteenth century, before there was street lighting, the richer people often employed men or boys to accompany them to their homes in the evenings after they had visited friends or been to the Assembly Room. These men were known as link-boys, because they carried torches of tow and pitch or wax or tallow which were known as links. Many houses had a narrow iron cone fitted to the railings into which the link-boy pushed his link in order to extinguish it. A few of these link extinguishers can still be seen.

Lock. See *Canal*

Lock-up. (Also known as the cage, the clink, the blind house, the round house and the house of correction.)

Before there were organized police forces, many villages had small lock-ups in which petty offenders were imprisoned for a day or two or where persons guilty of more serious crimes were placed until they could be transferred to the county gaol. The lock-up was under the care of the village beadle.

A number of these lock-ups still exist. Often they are circular in shape and for this reason are known as 'round houses'. Most of them appear to have been constructed in the eighteenth century and some have been scheduled as ancient monuments.

One lock-up, that at Bradford-on-Avon, Wiltshire, was originally an oratory. It stands on the town bridge and has a weather vane in the form of a fish, and this gave rise to the local saying that anybody who was imprisoned there was 'under the fish and over the water'. Another lock-up which may have been a chapel is at Lingfield, Surrey. It is shaped like a miniature church and was last used as a prison in 1882.

Neither of these can be regarded as typical lock-ups. The more usual type can be seen in the following villages:—

Steeple Ashton, Hilperton, and Shrewton in Wiltshire; Castle Cary and Monkton Combe in Somerset; Shenley in Hertfordshire; Alton in Staffordshire.

Log Floor. It is unusual for a floor to consist of the round sections of logs. Such a floor is to be found in the garden cottage in the National Trust garden at Killerton, near Exeter, where there is also a deer-bone floor (q.v.).

Long Barrow. This is a burial mound of the New Stone Age (2500–1900 B.C.). Many long barrows are between 200 and 300 feet in length—one near Maiden Castle in Dorset was one-third of a mile long, but this was exceptional. They are often more than 50 feet wide, but seldom above 8 feet high, although when originally constructed they were probably considerably higher. Sometimes they were merely mounds of earth, but often they consisted of long stone cairns and burial chambers, covered with earth. Usually the barrows have an east-west orientation and the east end, where the chamber is situated, is higher than the west. There is generally a ditch on either side of the barrow, but not at its ends.

Long barrows were normally used for more than one burial. In the earthen type a number of bodies were interred simultaneously, but the barrows with stone chambers were used for separate burials spread over a long period. The bodies were not cremated before burial.

Long barrows are fairly common in the west and south of England, particularly in Wiltshire, Hampshire, Dorset, and Somerset, and there are also examples in Yorkshire, Lincolnshire, and Wales. Among the best-preserved are Hetty Pegler's Tump, near Uley in Gloucestershire; and the long barrows at Stoney Littleton in Somerset; West Kennet in Wiltshire; Tinkinswood in Glamorgan; and Capel Barmon in Denbighshire.

Sometimes the earth covering the stone burial chamber has been removed, as at Kit's Coty House in Kent. The tomb is then known as a dolmen (q.v.).

Britain B.C., by S. E. Winbolt (Penguin Books, 1943)
A Guide to the Prehistoric and Roman Monuments in England and Wales, by Jacquetta Hawkes (Chatto and Windus, 1951)

Long-distance Footpaths. The National Parks Commission can propose to the Minister of Housing and Local Government that certain routes should be recognized as long-distance footpaths. These routes avoid roads used by vehicular traffic. Paths approved by the Minister include the Pennine Way (approximately 250 miles), the North Cornish Coast Path (135 miles) and the Pembrokeshire Coast Path (167 miles).

Lost Village. In the last six centuries about one thousand villages have disappeared. In some cases the disappearance is so thorough that their existence is known only from ancient documents or old maps. In other cases a few stones or some earthworks remain—mounds indicate the sites of houses and hollows show where there were roads. Aerial photography has brought many of these sites to light.

The inhabitants of these villages had been growers of cereal crops. Their villages disappeared because the owners of the land found a more profitable way of using it. By grazing sheep or cattle on the land they made much more money. They also decreased their labour costs because one or two men could care for a herd of animals grazing a considerable acreage, whereas many more were required to till the same amount of land.

When the thriving woollen industry of this country and of Western Europe made sheep-farming popular, many villagers were evicted, leaving only a shepherd or two and the lord of the manor. Often the latter, besides using much of the newly cleared land for grazing, used part of it to create beautiful parkland around a fine mansion, which he had built or enlarged with his recently gained wealth.

The change in the use of land was not the only reason for the disappearance of villages. A number on the coast were washed away; others were destroyed by fire. A few were depopulated by the Black Death.

Most depopulation took place in the fifteenth and sixteenth centuries. Later, in the seventeenth and eighteenth centuries, some villages were destroyed solely so that the owners of stately homes could surround them with parkland.

At only a few sites of lost villages has excavation taken place. They include Trewortha in Cornwall, Seacourt in Berkshire, Great Beere in Devonshire, and Wharram Percy in Yorkshire.

The Lost Villages of England, by Maurice Beresford (Lutter-
worth Press, 1954)

Lych-gate, or **Lich-gate.** The first part of this word is derived from the Anglo-Saxon *lic*, meaning a body. In olden days the corpse was rested on a table in the lych-gate before being taken into the church, and while it was there the priest read the first part of the burial service. Only the richer people were buried in coffins; the bodies of the poor were wrapped in sheets.

There are a few lych-gates which still possess coffin-tables, such as that at Chiddingfold in Surrey.

Old Crosses and Lych-gates, by Aymer Vallance (Batsford, 1920)

Lynchet. The people of the New Stone Age (2500-1900 B.C.) cultivated the slopes of the downs in terraces, which were separated from each other by little banks of earth. Often the traces of these banks can still be seen, although three thousand years or more have passed since they were first made. Their presence indicates that there was a settlement not far away.

It is not certain whether the lynchets were formed deliberately by the tillers of the land or whether they were the natural result of ploughing. When a sloping field is ploughed there is a tendency for the earth to creep slowly downwards and pile up at the lower edge.

M

Man-Wheel. See *Tread-wheel*

Marching Camp. It is remarkable to learn that we can still distinguish the sites of camps erected by the Roman legions when on the march, even though many of them were probably occupied for only one night. They are indicated by a shallow ditch and a low, rectangular vallum, or bank. The best-preserved ones are near Hadrian's Wall.

Mark Stone. The trackways used by the inhabitants of this country before the Romans came usually ran straight across the countryside, like the famous roads made by their conquerors. The ancient Britons maintained this alignment by setting up stones at various points along the tracks.

These stones were either unworked or only roughly chipped

into shape. Some of them were about twenty feet high, others only two or three feet. A few of the stones still remain; there is one beside a bridge at St Albans. In some cases they have been converted into churchyard crosses, or have been used as the bases of such crosses, as at Vowchurch in Herefordshire.

Market Cross. Among the best-known of the various types of crosses are those set up in present or former market-places, for they are to be found in towns and cities as well as in small villages. Some of them were originally preaching crosses (q.v.), but as their use for this purpose gradually declined, they were slowly given another function—that of marking the site on which people from the locality gathered to sell their produce. Some village crosses were erected to indicate the site of the market after the village's application to have a market of its own had been granted. In the Middle Ages any village more than six miles from a market had the right to make such an application.

Some market crosses, particularly those in villages, are quite simple affairs, like that at Ripley in Yorkshire; others, especially those in the towns, are more elaborate, like the crosses at Chichester, Salisbury, and Malmesbury. Some market crosses are known as butter crosses (q.v.).

Market Hall. Many towns possess old market halls. Often they are built on pillars, and stalls were placed in the space below the hall. Usually the hall was used for meetings, but sometimes buying and selling were transacted in it.

The fine hall at Shrewsbury in Shropshire was erected in 1596 and used as a market for flannel brought from Wales. The hall at Bridgnorth in the same county was once a barn.

Martello Tower. Martello towers were erected along the coasts of south-east England about the year 1804 as part of a system of coastal defence. At that time it was known that Napoleon was planning to invade the country.

The towers were between 30 and 40 feet high and had walls at least 6 feet thick. Each of them was garrisoned by small companies of not more than a dozen men, who lived in the upper part of the tower. The ground floor was used as a magazine. The tower's armament consisted of guns and howitzers on the roof. The entrance to the tower was usually a door about twenty feet above the ground, reached by a ladder which could be drawn up when all the men were inside. In some cases the tower was surrounded by a wide ditch which was crossed by a drawbridge.

The strange name of these towers was taken from a little-known victory gained by British troops over the French in 1794. Fourteen hundred soldiers were landed on Corsica with the object of capturing a tower which stood at Cape Martella. While they attacked the tower, the ships bombarded from the sea. The combined assault continued for nearly three hours without any sign of success, and it was not until a lucky shot set fire to the tower that its defences surrendered. Then the British troops were amazed to discover that they had been held off for so long by only two 18-pounders and one 6-pounder.

Mass Dial. See *Sundial*

Maypole. For many centuries the return of summer was welcomed by festivities on 1st May. The rejoicing commenced on the previous evening, when young men and girls went ' a-maying '. They wandered into the woods, ostensibly to gather flowers and branches and to welcome the dawn. In the morning they returned, laden with boughs and garlands, which were piled around the maypole on the village green and used to decorate the cottages. Then, throughout May Day, there were dancing and other festivities around the maypole. The Puritans halted these celebrations, for they said—quite truthfully—that the gathering of flowers and branches was by no means the only activity in which the young people indulged when they went ' a-maying '. After the Restoration the May Day dancing was revived, but the festivities were shorn of the immoralities with which they had previously been associated.

Today there are still some towns and villages which celebrate May Day, and a few of them proudly retain the maypole on the village green. One of these villages is Welford-on-Avon in

Warwickshire. A few places which no longer possess a maypole can point to a relic associated with it—a large stone with a hole in it in which the maypole was placed for support. Such a stone can be seen at Shalford in Surrey.

Maze. See *Turf Maze*

Megalithic Tomb. This type of tomb is an interesting relic of the New Stone Age (2500-1900 B.C.). It is a burial chamber intended for the interment of a number of bodies. The walls of the chamber, and sometimes the roof as well, were made of large blocks of stone, and the chamber itself was surmounted by a barrow or a cairn.

There are two main types of megalithic tomb—the passage grave, in which the burial chamber is approached by a narrow passage; and the gallery grave, which has no such passage. The passage grave is rare in England and Wales, although common in Scotland and Ireland. In fact, England does not possess a single example, and the only tombs of this type in Wales are in Anglesey, the best being at Bryn-Celli-Ddu, near Llanddaniel Fab.

The gallery graves are much commoner, but with the exception of a few in Kent they are all in the west of England or in Wales. They are of various types. Anglesey has examples of gallery graves, too; one of them is Bryn yr Hen Bobl, not far from the Menai Bridge.

A Guide to the Prehistoric and Roman Monuments in England and Wales, by Jacquetta Hawkes (Chatto and Windus, 1951)

Memorial Cross. Most of the crosses in our villages and towns were erected as preaching crosses or market crosses (q.v.), but a few were set up to commemorate an important local event or in memory of some local benefactor. One of the oldest of these memorial crosses is at Barton in Yorkshire. It was erected over a thousand years ago by the monks of Lindisfarne to mark one of the places at which they stayed when they fled before the Danish invaders, carrying with them the body of

St Cuthbert. Among the best-known memorial crosses are those set up at the places where the body of Queen Eleanor rested during its last journey. (See *Eleanor Cross*)

Menhir. This is a single upright stone erected in Neolithic times (2500-1900 B.C.). The name comes from two Celtic words, *maen* meaning high and *hir* meaning stone. Menhirs are the commonest type of ancient stone monument and are found on the moorlands of the west and north of England. Most of them seem to have been erected as single upright stones, although there is a possibility that a few are the sole survivors of the stones used to construct larger monuments. The reason for their erection is unknown, and various suggestions have been put forward as to the purpose they served—that they were gravestones, that they marked a boundary, that they commemorated some person or event, or that they had an astronomical purpose. Menhirs are also known as monoliths and standing stones.

Milecastle. Along Hadrian's Wall, at intervals of one Roman mile, there were small forts, the largest of which was about 70 feet long and 60 feet wide. Each fort could accommodate about a hundred men. The lower walls of many of these milecastles still remain.

Handbook to the Roman Wall, by J. Collingwood Bruce (Longmans, Green, 10th edition, 1947)

Milestone. The first milestones in this country were erected by the Romans. They are believed to have measured all their distances from the *Miliarium Aureum*, or ' Golden milestone ', now known as the London Stone, which is let into the wall of St Swithin's Church in Cannon Street, London. The only Roman milestone still in its original position is at Stanegate in Northumberland.

After the departure of the Romans no milestones appear to have been set up until the eighteenth century. During the sixteenth century a Cambridge don had bequeathed £1,600 to Trinity Hall and directed that the interest was to be used for repairing the sixteen miles of road between Barkway and Cambridge. In 1727 the Master of Trinity College decided that some of the money should be used to meet the cost of placing milestones on this stretch of road. The stones set up were only small, and in 1731 they were replaced by larger ones, a few of which still remain. They all bear the black crescent of Trinity Hall.

In 1766 the provision of milestones was made compulsory by the passing of the General Turnpike Act. The purpose of this was to prevent overcharging by carriers. The distances shown on many old milestones are incorrect; in some cases this inaccuracy was deliberate. For example, the reigning monarch used to be expected to take one of his cabinet ministers with him whenever he travelled more than fifty miles from London. George IV found this rule particularly irksome, for he liked to pay frequent visits to Brighton, which was fifty-two miles away. It was therefore arranged that all the milestones should show the distance as less than fifty miles!

On the road between London and Eastbourne there are a number of milestones made of iron which bear no words but only the number of miles and a bow with four bells suspended from it, indicating that they show the distance from Bow Bells. At the top of some of these milestones there is a small buckle. This is the Pelham Buckle, the badge of a famous Sussex family.

Other particularly interesting milestones are the Dick Whittington milestone at the foot of Highgate Hill, London; the ' Shy Milestone ' at West Wycombe, Bucks, which is so called because although it gives the distance to London, Oxford, and Aylesbury it mentions none of them by name, but refers to them as ' The City ', ' The University ' and ' The County Town '; and England's tallest milestone, more than 50 feet high, which is at Chalfont St Peter, Bucks.

Military Bridge. The name ' military bridge ' is normally reserved for the structures made by General Wade in the eighteenth century, when he was commander-in-chief in Scotland and was ordered to build roads to connect the Highland garrisons. Of the forty bridges which he built as part of this task very few remain. The finest is at Aberfeldy, in Perthshire.

Miniature Village. See *Model Village*

Mist Pond. See *Dew Pond*

Mock Window. See *Trompe L'Oeil Window*

Model Village. There are in England a number of miniature villages, most of which are the result of several years of devoted work by one or two enthusiasts. One of the best-known is ' Bekonscot ' at Beaconsfield. It has a miniature railway, with toy engines, and a miniature airport.

In some of these villages adherence to the same scale throughout has presented difficulties. For example, the model inhabitants are too large or too small when compared with the size of the buildings, or real plants, used as trees, are out of all proportion to the buildings.

This problem was tackled in the miniature village at Bourton-on-the-Water in Gloucestershire. There the model, carefully built to scale, is a copy of Bourton itself. Its construction occupied eight men for four years.

There are other miniature villages at Ripley in Surrey and at Hornsea in Yorkshire. A charge is made for admission to most of these villages, but in several cases the profits are given to charity.

Monolith. See *Menhir*

Moon Dial. Sundials are fairly common, but moon dials are extremely rare. There is one at Eyam in Derbyshire.

Moot Hall. In some places the town hall (q.v.) is still known as the moot hall. The moot was the name given in Saxon times to the assembly of representatives of the hundred, which was a sub-division of the shire.

Moot Stone. In a few villages a stone around which the moot held its meetings can still be seen. There is a moot stone at Toseland in Huntingdonshire.

Mounting Block. A mounting block or upping block consists of a flight of three or four steps formed by placing flat stones of different lengths one upon the other. Their purpose was to enable those who were not very agile to mount their horses or alight from their coaches without difficulty. They are usually found near such buildings as churches and inns, which were visited by a large number of people travelling on horseback or by coach. There is one outside the church at Herstmonceux in Sussex, and another outside the public house at Winsley in Wiltshire.

Movable Bridge. There are various types of movable bridge, ranging from small ones on the canals to much larger structures operated by machinery. The best-known is, of course, London's Tower Bridge. Others include the Barton Swing Aqueduct, which carries the Bridgewater Canal over the Manchester Ship Canal, and the Newport Lifting Bridge at Middlesbrough, which lifts a road so that ships can pass underneath.

Museum. The ancient Egyptians opened the first museum, but in this country museums were almost unknown until the seventeenth century, when a few wealthy men made collections of objects of interest and bequeathed them for public use. The best-known of these collections is probably that amassed by Elias Ashmole; it formed the basis of the Ashmolean Museum at Oxford.

The number of museums remained small until the second half of the nineteenth century, when the increased facilities for education and the widespread desire for knowledge led to the establishment of many museums. Today there are over eight hundred in Britain; some of them are in imposing buildings in our large cities, while others are in single rooms in small towns and consist almost entirely of objects of local interest.

(See also *Folk Museum*)

The Museum: its History and its Tasks in Education, by A. S. Wittlin (Kegan Paul, 1949)

N

National Park. A national park is an area of countryside which is protected by law from exploitation in order to preserve it for public enjoyment.

In 1945 the Government published a White Paper outlining a plan for National Parks and set up a committee to consider these proposals. This committee, which reported in 1947, recommended the establishment of twelve National Parks over a period of three years in instalments of four each year, beginning with the Lake District, North Wales, the Peak District, and Dartmoor.

The report was followed by the passing of the National Parks and Access to the Countryside Act, which became law in December, 1949. It authorized the setting up of a commission to advise on steps to be taken to preserve and enhance natural beauty, particularly in National Parks and ' areas of outstanding natural beauty ', and to recommend the creation of long-distance footpaths and methods to be taken to improve the behaviour of visitors to the countryside. The commission's powers are almost entirely advisory; it cannot designate which areas shall be National Parks, but can only make recommendations on the matter to the Minister of Housing and Local Government.

Areas so far designated as National Parks include the Peak District, the Lake District, Snowdonia, Dartmoor, the Pembrokeshire Coast, and the North Yorks Moors.

The Act states that if a park is entirely in the area of one planning authority it shall be administered by that authority, one third of whose planning committee shall be appointed by the Minister. (The planning authorities are the county and county borough councils.) Where a park is in the area of two or more authorities it shall be administered by a joint board. The Minister decides how many representatives each of the authorities shall appoint to the board and in what proportion they shall contribute to its expenses. In special circumstances, instead of setting up a joint board, the Minister may allow each planning authority to continue to administer the part of the park within its area. If he decides to do this, a joint advisory committee has to be set up to advise the planning authorities. One third of the members of every joint board and joint advisory committee are appointed by the Minister.

Annual Reports of the National Parks Commission (H.M.S.O.) Some of the Park Boards have also published reports.

Nature Reserve. A nature reserve is an area protected from building development in order to preserve its vegetation or to provide a sanctuary for birds or animals. Prior to 1949, when the National Parks and Access to the Countryside Act became law, the protection of nature reserves was undertaken by the National Trust, local authorities, or various private organizations. The Act empowered the Nature Conservancy to establish nature reserves, and among those so far designated by the Conservancy are Kingley Vale in Sussex, noted for its yew trees; Castor Hanglands in Northamptonshire, well-known for rare butterflies; and Bridgwater Bay, on the Somerset coast, a sanctuary for geese and waders. The official name for a nature reserve is a *conservation area*.

Nesting Box. See *Pigeon Hole*.

Nine Men's Morris Board. Nine men's morris was once a popular pastime. It was a game for two players, each of whom had nine men or pieces. The lines drawn on the board met or crossed at twenty-four points, and each player took it in turns to place his nine pieces on these points and then move them from one vacant point to another. When a player had three pieces in an unbroken row, he was entitled to take one of his opponent's men, and the game continued until one player had only two pieces left. A stone with a nine men's morris board

Part of the model village at Beaconsfield, Buckinghamshire

A mounting block outside a Wiltshire farmhouse

Palladian bridge, Prior Park, Bath

cut on it is built into the wall of the church at Sparsholt in Berkshire.

O

Ogam (or **Ogham**) **Stone.** This is a standing stone inscribed with the Ogam script, which was a system of strokes placed at various angles to a long base line. It was widely used in the fifth century A.D., particularly in Ireland. There are Ogam stones at Lewannick in Cornwall.

P

Packhorse Bridge. In the Middle Ages merchandise was usually transported in panniers on the back of pack-horses. These horses travelled along the bridle-paths and roads in single file, and in places bridges were erected which were just wide enough for one horse to cross at a time. Some of these bridges remain. Most of them are simple, picturesque structures with only one arch, but Wycoller in Lancashire possesses a twin-arched bridge which was built in the thirteenth century. It seems that pack-horse transport was more widely used in Lancashire and York-shire than in other parts of the country, for these counties have a fair number of pack-horse bridges. On the other hand, Wales possesses very few of them, although one, at Dinas Mawddwy, in Merioneth, also has two arches. The use of pack-horses continued long after the Middle Ages and by no means all of the pack-horse bridges date from that period.

There is one near Otley in Yorkshire which was built in 1738.

Palladian Bridge. This rare type of bridge—decorative, with a roof supported by pillars—was erected on the estates of a few wealthy landowners in the eighteenth century. It takes its name from Palladio, an Italian architect. There are Palladian bridges at Wilton Park in Wiltshire and at Prior Park, Bath.

Paper Glove. See *Funeral Garland*

Pauper Grave. Although pauper burials—burials at the expense of the parish—were once far too common, in only a few places is it possible to distinguish the graves of the paupers from those of the more fortunate members of the community. At Ormskirk in Lancashire they were buried in a certain part of the churchyard and on the tombstones were inscribed not their names, but the name of the village from which they came— *Upholland Poor, Formy Poor,* etc.

Pavement Bollard. When all vehicles were horse-drawn, pillars were sometimes erected on the edges of pavements at corners in towns in order to prevent the horses from cutting across the corners. These pillars were about three feet high. There are some near the centre of Birmingham.

Peat Track. Many of the hillside paths in the Lake District were originally the tracks used by the local inhabitants to bring peat from the moors which lie high up between the dales. These tracks, which had a surface of turf laid on stone, were about seven feet wide, to allow the sledges used for hauling peat to pass along them. The men carried these sledges on their backs to the peat bogs and then sent them down loaded with the fuel. The men had to run in front of the sledges to check their speed. Some of the stone sheds used to store the peat near the bogs still remain.

Peel Tower or **Pele Tower.** In the days when raids between England and Scotland were frequent, towers were built on both sides of the border as places of refuge for the local inhabitants. They were known as peel towers because each of them was usually surrounded by a wooden fence, called a peel. Most of them were of three or four storeys. The ground floor was often used as a store-room. The first floor was the main hall of the building, where meals were cooked and eaten, whilst the upper storeys were used as sleeping quarters.

Northumberland has a number of peel towers, some of which have been converted into farmhouses or dwellings. Cockle Park Tower at Hebron is a fifteenth-century tower which is now a farmhouse. Shortflatt Tower at Bolam, built in the previous century, forms part of a dwelling-house. At Belsay there is a peel tower attached to the castle. Corbridge has two peel towers: one was built in the late fifteenth century and has a house attached; the other, known as the Vicar's Pele, is in the churchyard. The last peel tower erected before the Union of England and Scotland is at Doddington; it was built in 1584.

On the other side of the border there are also many peel towers, most of them now in ruins. They are notable for the thickness of their walls—often between six and ten feet—and their otherwise small dimensions. The outer measurements of the tower at Barns, near Peebles, are 28 feet by 28 feet; when the thickness of the walls is deducted, it will be seen that the rooms were certainly not large. Barns possesses a feature which seems to be peculiar to the Scottish towers. This is an iron grating over the doorway, forming an additional protection if the door itself was destroyed. Other Scottish peel towers can be seen at Ferniehurst near Jedburgh, at Newark in Selkirkshire, and at Closeburn in Dumfriesshire.

Pest House. Some town and villages used to have pest houses in which, before the days of hospitals, very sick people, especially those suffering from infectious diseases, were placed. Often they were left there to die, and for this reason the pest house was usually close to a burial ground. A few pest houses still remain; one is in the churchyard at Odiham in Hampshire.

Pier. This name is given to various types of seaside structure, including landing stages, jetties, and works built to shelter harbours, but the best-known kind of pier is undoubtedly that at seaside resorts. This, in addition to being a promenade and amusement centre for holiday-makers, is also sometimes a landing stage.

Promenade piers are usually built on open pile work of timber or steel, although recently reinforced concrete has also been used. The open type of construction has two advantages over a more solid kind of erection—the drift of sand along the coast is not interfered with, and the surface exposed to the waves is comparatively small.

In the early years of the nineteenth century, when seaside holidays first became really popular, there was great rivalry between the resorts. One matter in which there was fierce competition was the construction of elaborate and expensive piers. Margate spent £100,000 to rebuild the pier there after it was damaged in a storm in 1808. Brighton, however, was probably the resort which possessed the most famous pier. This was the chain pier, which was completed in 1823. It was one of the earliest piers to have sideshows and machines like those which are now a feature of all piers. For the first sixteen years its only attraction of this nature was a camera obscura, but in 1839 a weighing machine was added which recorded the name and weight of every person using it. This pier was destroyed in a gale in 1896. A storm was also responsible for the destruction in 1951 of what was probably the only remaining chain pier—that at Seaview, Isle of Wight.

Pigeon Hole, or **Nesting Box.** Up to the reign of Elizabeth I only lords of the manor and priests were allowed to keep pigeons, and many of them had dovecotes for this purpose. When pigeon-keeping ceased to be a privilege, other people sometimes had pigeon holes made in the walls of their houses, such as those to be seen in the Gloucestershire village of Duntisbourne Leer. At Bradmore, Notts, there are over two hundred pigeon holes in one of the end walls of a barn.

Pillory. The pillory was an instrument of punishment consisting of a wooden frame with holes through which the head and hands of the offender were placed. It was rather more uncomfortable than the stocks (q.v.) because the culprit had to stand throughout the period of punishment, whereas the stocks were provided with a seat. Whilst he was pilloried or in the stocks the wrongdoer was at the mercy of the populace, who could ridicule him or throw refuse at him.

Until 1637 it was used as a punishment for such offences as forgery, perjury, and cornering the market and putting up the price of goods. In 1637 a law was passed forbidding the printing or publishing of books without a licence. This was a form of press censorship, the aim of which was to stop the issue of pamphlets attacking the government. The law decreed that offenders should be pilloried, and among those who suffered in this way was Daniel Defoe.

The pillory fell into disuse during the second half of the eighteenth century and it was abolished as a means of punishment in 1837. One of the last pillories to be used was that which is still preserved at Rye, where an offender was pilloried in 1813.

A number of other pillories still survive. That at Coleshill, in Warwickshire, can accommodate two offenders and is also fitted with a whipping post. There is a pillory in the parish church at Ashby-de-la-Zouch, Leicestershire, which was designed to grip the prisoner by the wrists.

Pinfold. See *Pound*

Pitch-pipe. In the days before organs were installed in churches, the pitch for singing was often provided by the clerk, who blew the note on a pipe at the commencement of each hymn or psalm. Some churches still possess a pitch-pipe; there is one at Aldbury in Hertfordshire.

Plague Stone. When some villages found themselves stricken by the dreaded plague which ravaged large parts of the country from time to time, they often heroically isolated themselves from the rest of the world. People from neighbouring towns and villages would bring them food, which they would leave in a certain spot—often on a large stone—on the outskirts of the affected village. The inhabitants of this village would then collect the food, leaving the money for it in a receptacle containing vinegar, in order that the infection should not be conveyed by means of the coins.   There is a plague stone at Alford in Lincolnshire.

Pond Barrow.   See *Round Barrow*

Ports.   See *Former Ports*

Pound.   (1) The pound, or pinfold, was a very small piece of enclosed land, usually not more than twenty square yards in area, in which stray animals were impounded.   If a man found somebody else's cattle on his land he could seize them and remove them to the pound, where they were kept until the owner paid for the damage they had done.   Pounds were necessary because farm land was frequently unfenced, so that animals often strayed, causing damage to other people's property.   Many towns and villages appointed one of their menfolk to look after the animals in the pound; he was known as the pinder.

Some pounds still remain, although they are no longer used. There are two at Godalming in Surrey.   These are the usual shape—square—but at Wrentham and Freckenham in Suffolk there are circular pounds.

Pound.   (2) On Dartmoor the ruin of the wall which was sometimes built around a group of hut circles is known as a pound. (See *Hut Circle*)

Preaching Cross.   The first Christian missionaries often erected crosses at the places where they preached the Christian faith. Frequently these crosses were set up on the sites of pagan shrines.   Sometimes a church was later built near the cross, and that is why many of these preaching crosses are now inside churchyards.   Two fine crosses at Sandbach in Cheshire are more than thirteen hundred years old; during the Puritan era they suffered the fate of many preaching crosses and were destroyed.   Fortunately all the parts were later found and the crosses were carefully reconstructed.

Not all the preaching crosses date from the beginning of Christianity in this country.   In the Middle Ages crosses were often set up by preaching friars when they were forbidden to preach in churches by the parish priests, who were jealous of the popularity achieved by the friars. Many of these crosses are mounted on platforms reached by flights of steps; it was on these platforms that the friars stood when preaching the gospel.

There is a fifteenth-century cross at Great Malvern. Like a number of other medieval crosses it has a niche in the shaft. The purpose of these niches is not known.

(See also *Churchyard Cross*)

Old Crosses and Lych-gates, by Aymer Vallance (Batsford, 1920)

Priest's Hole. During the religious persecutions of Tudor times secret hiding places were built in many large houses. These hiding places were frequently used by Catholic priests, and so they came to be known as priests' holes.

Many of them were constructed by a Jesuit lay-brother named Nicholas Owen, who was also a carpenter. He had to make each one differently, otherwise the discovery of one would have led to the finding of others. Among the priests' holes which he made were several at Hindlip Hall, near Worcester, and there came a time when he himself had to take refuge in one of them. After hiding for about a week, he left the secret room and was immediately captured, taken to London, and executed.

There are many hiding places at Compton Wynyates in Warwickshire and a priest's hole has also been found at Sulgrave Manor in Northamptonshire, the home of George Washington's ancestors.

Priest's House. See *Clergy House*

Public Library. There were libraries in Assyria and ancient Egypt; the latter country possessed the greatest library of ancient times at Alexandria. The first Roman public library was established during the reign of Augustus.

In Saxon times many monasteries had libraries, but these consisted almost entirely of manuscripts written by the monks themselves. The Church continued the voluntary work of collecting and safeguarding books throughout the Middle Ages. The catalogues of many of the monastic libraries have been preserved, and because of this we know that the monastery of Christ Church, Canterbury, possessed three thousand books.

The books were usually arranged on lectern desks or in bookcases, to which they were fastened by chains. A complete chained library can still be seen in Hereford Cathedral, and a number of churches possess chained Bibles or other chained books. Among them are St Helen's Church at Abingdon in Berkshire, and the church at Cumnor in the same county.

The invention of printing made possible the development of the library movement as we know it, but it was not until the middle of the seventeenth century that the first free library in England was opened. This was probably the Chetham Library at Manchester, which was established in 1653. Scotland's oldest lending library was also opened about three centuries ago. It can still be visited at Innerpeffray in Perthshire. Like many other early libraries, it was established by a local benefactor.

During the eighteenth century subscription libraries and circulating libraries enjoyed wide popularity. Local authorities were authorized by the Public Libraries (England) Act of 1850 to use money from the rates to open and maintain public libraries, but for some years only a small number of councils took advantage of this law. Similar legislation in respect of Scotland and Ireland was passed in 1853. A great impetus was given to the public library movement by the millionaire Andrew Carnegie, who spent £1,250,000 on presenting library buildings to towns and cities.

The Medieval Library, by J. W. Thompson (Cambridge University Press, 1939)

The Chained Library, by B. H. Streeter (Macmillan, 1931)

A History of the Public Library Movement in Great Britain and Ireland, by J. Minto (Allen and Unwin, 1932)

The Public Library, by W. J. Murison (Harrap, 1955)

Pump. See *Village Pump* and *Wayside Pump*

Pump-house. In many villages the inhabitants used to have to obtain their water from a communal pump or spring. (See *Village Pump*.) Sometimes a shelter, known as a pump-house, was erected to give protection from the weather to the people while they were fetching their water. Among the villages which possess a pump-house is Great Budworth in Cheshire.

Q

Quintain. Tilting the quintain formed a popular part of knightly tournaments in the Middle Ages. The quintain consisted of a post with a bar at the top which turned on a pivot. A flat board was fitted to one end of the bar and a bag of sand to the other. Each rider taking part in the sport had to gallop along and strike the board with his lance and then pass on before the sandbag swung round and struck him on the back or head. If he was unfortunate enough to be hit in this way the force of the blow was often sufficient to unhorse him.

Today there is only one quintain still standing in its original position. This is on the village green at Offham in Kent.

Quoit is the name given in Cornwall and in parts of Wales to a dolmen (q.v.).

R

'Recumbent Stone' Circle. This type of prehistoric monument is found in the north-east of Scotland. The upright stones, instead of being of uniform height, gradually increase in size towards one side of the circle, and between the tallest pair of stones there is a recumbent slab. In the middle of the circle there was a small cairn which marked the burial place of the cremated remains of deceased persons. These circles date from the Early Bronze Age.

Reservoir. When it is desired to store up the water in part of a river instead of allowing all of it to flow onwards to the sea, a wall of masonry is built across the valley. This wall is known as a dam (q.v.). The area of water impounded by the dam is called a reservoir. The water may be used to generate electricity or to irrigate the surrounding land, or it may be conveyed to a distant community for domestic purposes.

Care has to be taken in deciding the site for a reservoir. If a position high up in the mountains is chosen the quantity of water is likely to vary greatly according to the rainfall. On the other hand, the site must not be too low, because then it may not be possible to maintain sufficient pressure.

A reservoir to supply London with water was built at Clerkenwell in 1613 and a little over a century later two more were constructed in Hyde Park and St James's Park. They were very small compared with modern reservoirs. The largest reservoir in the country is now the Ladybower Reservoir in Derbyshire; it has an area of 504 acres.

Rhine. In the low-lying countryside around Glastonbury in Somerset fields are often separated by wide ditches instead of by walls or hedges. This type of ditch is known as a rhine (pronounced *reen*).

Road. The first tracks were made not by men but by animals as they regularly followed the same paths to the ponds from which they drank. Then the need to barter goods led the early inhabitants of this country to form tracks between the communities in which they lived. Often these routes followed the hilltops, because there sudden attack was less likely. Consequently they were known as ridgeways, and one of these ancient tracks is still called the Ridgeway. The constant use of some tracks resulted in a gradual wearing down of the soil, so that a depression was formed ; these tracks were known as hollow ways. It was not only trade which brought about the formation of roads. Religion, too, played an important part, and many of the tracks led to temples such as Avebury. To all these ancient routes the name of green road is usually given.

The tracks often went from one landmark to another. If there was no suitable natural landmark, then the path was frequently indicated by placing a boulder beside it; such a boulder is known as a mark stone (q.v.).

The first real roads in this country were, of course, the work of the Romans, who constructed roads primarily for military purposes. Where it was convenient to do so, they made their roads follow the existing tracks; where this was not suitable, entirely new routes were constructed. The main highways were maintained by the government, while the upkeep of the less important routes was the responsibility of the local inhabitants. (See *Roman Road*)

The Saxons allowed the fine Roman roads to fall into disrepair. They had no great need for an elaborate system of highways, for few of them journeyed far from their native villages, and there was little trade. Furthermore, they did not know how to shoe horses, and the hard surface of the Roman roads was quite unsuitable for their unshod animals.

In the first two centuries following the Norman invasion the roads continued to be neglected, for the only people to travel at all widely were soldiers. Travel by ordinary citizens was dangerous because of the large number of desperate fugitives who lived in the forests and woodlands. Edward I attempted to make travel safer by ordering all parishes to ensure that the trees and bushes within two hundred feet of a highway were cut down, but in many places this law was ignored. In medieval times wealthy monasteries often constructed and maintained roads because the monks had to travel between the various monastic estates. In the reign of Edward III tolls were levied on some roads to pay for their repair. The state of most of the roads was so bad that transport by any form of vehicle was almost impossible and merchandise had to be conveyed by pack-horses.

During the sixteenth century there was a great increase in commercial activity and this led to the roads being used by a far greater amount of traffic. Following the fashion of Queen Elizabeth I, people travelled for pleasure as well as for business, and the need for improvements to the roads became obvious to all. In 1555 Parliament passed an Act making each parish responsible for the maintenance of its highways and requiring every able-bodied male villager to spend six days each year repairing the roads. The parish authorities had to appoint a road surveyor; this post was unpaid and was held for twelve months, after which another surveyor was chosen. The surveyors had to report on the state of the roads, but since they were, of course, untrained, their reports were not of very great value. Needless to say, the six days' voluntary labour did not lead to any great improvements.

Parliament next decided to tackle the problem in a different way. Instead of repairing the roads, they thought that they would prevent further deterioration by limiting the size of the vehicles travelling on them, and in 1621 an Act came into force making it illegal to use four-wheeled vehicles or wagons with a load weighing more than one ton.

This method of dealing with the matter was, of course, quite unsatisfactory and in 1663 the first Turnpike Act was passed. It provided for tolls to be collected from every traveller using a stretch of road in Hertfordshire; the money was to be used for the maintenance of the road. A toll-house was erected and a barrier placed across the road in front of it. (See *Toll-house*)

In the eighteenth century a long series of similar Acts empowered bodies known as Turnpike Trusts to build and maintain roads by means of tolls collected on them. Measures were taken to ensure that the toll-keepers handed over the money they received, but the existence of the Trusts did not lead to any great improvements, for a method of constructing good roads was still unknown.

The eighteenth century saw the building of the first real highways since the departure of the Romans. After the Jacobite rebellion of 1715 General Wade was appointed Commander-in-Chief in Scotland, and in order that his troops could move quickly from one part of the country to another he constructed some good roads. Like the Romans, he realized that solid foundations were essential. The governments in England were very pleased with his work, but did not copy his example, and the continual bad state of the roads led to serious riots against the Turnpike Trusts.

Then, in the second half of the century, a blind man showed the country how roads should be made. He was John Metcalf —'Blind Jack' of Knaresborough. He persuaded the local officials to allow him to rebuild a stretch of road near his native town, and his work was so good that other authorities employed him. Before his death in 1810 he had constructed about two hundred miles of road.

Two other road-builders, both Scotsmen, built many miles of good highways in the first half of the nineteenth century. John Loudon Macadam's roads were made of a layer of broken stones a foot deep, without any loose material, so that vehicles passing over them packed them tighter and tighter together. Thomas Telford built nearly a thousand miles of road in Scotland as well as constructing the main highway from London to Holyhead. He aimed to make his roads last for many years, and with this in view he gave them a foundation of stone blocks. On top of these there was a layer of small stones, and then a gravel surface three inches deep.

Meanwhile the number of turnpikes had increased until there were about eight thousand of them. In South Wales they were the cause of the Rebecca Riots, in which gangs of men dressed as women smashed the gates during the hours of darkness. In the latter half of the century Parliament took steps to reduce the number of toll-roads.

Although the work of Metcalf, Macadam, and Telford had led to tremendous improvements in the roads, these highways were not able to stand up to the heavy increase in traffic which followed the invention of the motor-car. The pneumatic tyres tended to dislodge the broken stones with which the macadamized roads were constructed, leaving holes which soon filled with water, so that large ruts were formed. In dry weather the tyres also sucked up the loose dust, so that each vehicle was followed by a thick cloud. This dust problem was tackled by spraying tar on the surface of the roads.

The motor traffic led to the need for constant repairs and improvements to the roads and this placed a heavy financial burden on local authorities. To help to meet the cost the Road Fund was started; this consisted of the revenue from motor licences. To ensure that the best use was made of this money, the Road Board was set up in 1910, with power to construct new highways or to make grants to local authorities for the improvement of existing roads. During the four years preceding the outbreak of war, the Board did much good work.

In 1919 its duties were taken over by the newly-formed Ministry of Transport, which had to remedy the neglect of the war years and also cope with the greatly increased amount of traffic. It became obvious that new materials for road construction were required; continual patching of the old surfaces was quite inadequate. Tarmacadam was chosen as the most suitable substance; it consists of road metal of which every piece is coated with tar. A thick layer is spread over the road and rolled in. Other materials are bitumen and concrete.

Today the Ministry of Transport and Civil Aviation continues to be responsible for supervising the maintenance of the roads, although, of course, direct responsibility for many of them falls on local authorities. Unfortunately only a small part of the enormous sum contributed in taxation by motorists has been made available for road improvements, and this has until recently prevented any large-scale measures for the construction of motorways to ease the terrible traffic problem.

The Ancient Roads of England, by Jane Oliver (Cassell, 1936)

The Story of Britain's Highways, by Ronald Syme (Pitman, 1952)

The Story of the King's Highway, by Sidney and Beatrice Webb (Longmans, 1913)

The Story of the Road, by J. W. Gregory (MacLehose, 1931)

From Track to By-pass, by T. W. Wilkinson (Methuen, 1934)

Rock Carving. The people of the Bronze Age (1900–450 B.C.,) sometimes made carvings on boulders. By far the commonest form of carving was the cup and ring marking (q.v.). These carvings almost certainly had some religious significance, but it is unlikely that their real meaning will ever be known. There are many of them near Doddington in Northumberland.

Rock Grave. Why anybody should undertake the hard task of scooping graves from the living rock when they could have been dug much more easily in softer soil nearby is a mystery. Yet that is what happened at Heysham in Lancashire, where there are a number of tombs cut in the rock on the edge of a cliff. The covers and contents of eight of them have disappeared. Each of them is shaped for the body and the head, and has a socket in which a wooden cross was placed. They are believed to be nine hundred years old.

Roman Amphitheatre. Most Romans towns had an amphitheatre just outside their walls. Good examples can be seen at Cirencester and at Caerleon. Dorchester's amphitheatre, known as Maumbury Rings, had originally been constructed as a religious sanctuary in the New Stone Age or the Bronze Age; the Romans converted it to serve purposes of entertainment.

The amphitheatre usually had an oval arena surrounded by banks formed of the earth which was removed in excavating the arena. On these banks were the seats for the spectators. Caerleon's amphitheatre had an arena about 200 feet long and 150 feet wide, with eight entrances. There was room for about six thousand spectators.

Roman Bath. By far the finest remains of Roman public baths are those at Bath, in Somerset. Even in Roman times Bath was a spa, bearing the name *Aquae Sulis*—the waters of the goddess Sul. The natural hot springs provided warm water for the luxury-loving Romans' swimming baths. The largest bath was an open-air swimming pool 80 feet long and 40 feet wide. The medicinal value of the waters attracted people not only from other parts of Roman Britain, but also from Gaul and other countries in Western Europe.

Roman Fort. The remains of a Roman fort can be distinguished from those of a prehistoric fort by its straight sides. Usually Roman forts were quadrangular, with a gate in the centre of each side. Most of them were along the boundaries with Wales and Scotland or in south-eastern England—the Saxon Shore. Sometimes a considerable amount of the Roman stonework remains, as at Portchester in Hampshire and Pevensey in Sussex. (The Normans later chose both these places to be the sites of castles.)

Roman Road. A number of modern roads follow the same route as Roman roads, and consequently the Roman road is buried. There are, however, the remains of some Roman roads still visible. Usually it is only the centre of the road which can be seen, but occasionally the ditches or banks at the side have also been preserved.

The first step taken by the Romans when constructing a road was, of course, to survey the route which it was to follow. As is well known, long stretches of road ran across the country-side in a straight line. After the route had been determined, trenches were dug at each side, usually about 22 Roman feet apart. These served in the first instance to mark the course of the road and then were later made into ditches for drainage purposes. The site was excavated and filled in with a bed of material, on which was placed the surface layers.

The metalling consisted of the materials most readily available. In the south of England this was usually a mixture of gravel, chalk and small stones, as in the well-preserved stretch

Quintain, Offham, Kent

Teazle Tower, Woodchester, Gloucestershire

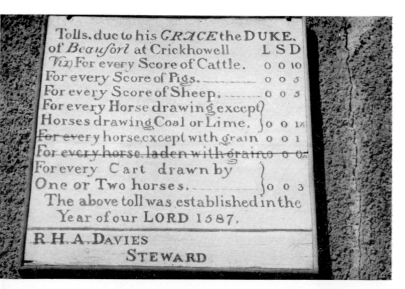

Tollboard, Crickhowell, Breconshire

Stocks, near Leigh, Kent

Village sign, Thursley, Surrey

of road near Badbury Rings in Dorset. In the Weald of Kent and Sussex slag from the iron furnaces was used; a short stretch of a road of this type can be seen at Holtye in Sussex. In the north of England stone paving is found, as at Blackstone Edge above Littleborough in Yorkshire.

Roman Roads in Britian, by Ivan D. Margary (Phoenix House, 1955)

Roman Roads in Britain, by T. Codrington (S.P.C.K., 1903, 1918)

Roman Signal Station. At various points around the coast the Romans erected coastguard, or signal, stations. A square walled enclosure, with turrets at the corners, was surrounded by a ditch. In the centre of the enclosure stood a wooden tower, built on a square stone foundation. This tower was 80 or 100 feet high. About forty men lived in each signal station.

Remains of signal stations can be seen on Castle Hill, Scarborough, and at Goldsborough, near Whitby.

Britain Under the Romans, by S. E. Winbolt (Penguin Books, 1945)

Roman Theatre. The Romans constructed very few theatres in Britain. The remains of one at St Albans were excavated in 1934 and are now open to the public. This theatre was built about A.D. 140 and twice reconstructed. It was an open-air theatre with a tier of seats forming a large segment of a circle, with a small stage and an arena. Behind the stage were the dressing-rooms, the only part of the structure to have a roof.

The Roman Theatre at Verulamium, by A. W. G. Lowther (The Marchand Press)

Roman Town. Most of the towns constructed by the Romans have long since been built over. All of them were laid out on a fairly regular system of straight streets, and contained such

G

public buildings as a market, a public bath, and a basilica—
the Roman equivalent of the town hall.

The most spectacular site of a Roman town is at St Albans.
Other interesting sites are at Silchester in Hampshire, which,
unlike the remainder, has not been built upon, but is now
farmland; Caerwent in Monmouthshire; and Cirencester in
Gloucestershire. Cirencester was the second largest town in
Roman Britain, its size being exceeded only by that of London,
which had an area of 325 acres. Most of the Roman towns
were small ; Silchester, for example, with an area of 120 acres,
probably had a population of less than four thousand.

Britain Under the Romans, by S. E. Winbolt (Penguin Books,
1945)
Roman Britain, by I. A. Richmond (Penguin Books, 1955)

Roman Villa. In the south of England there are the remains
of a number of villas built during the Roman occupation. The
term ' villa ' is used to describe a variety of structures, ranging
from farm-houses to large residences of wealthy Romans. By
no means all of them belonged to Romans; many were the
property of British farmers and land-owners.

The earliest villas were simple single-storey structures with
four or five rooms. The later villas fall into four main types.

The first was built around a courtyard; there is an example
of a large courtyard house at Northleigh in Oxfordshire. There
were buildings along three sides of the courtyard, while the
fourth side had a wall with a gateway. The best rooms were
in the central portion, which was rebuilt several times before
the villa was finally abandoned. Usually in villas of the courtyard type one wing was the servants' quarters and the other
was used as workshops.

The second kind of villa was the corridor house. It had no
courtyard and the rooms opened on to a corridor. A villa of
this type has been discovered at Mansfield Woodhouse in
Nottinghamshire.

A combination of the courtyard house and the corridor

house, with one corridor adjacent to the courtyard and another on the side of the house farthest from the courtyard is to be seen on the cliffs at Folkestone, where there are two villas of this type.

The fourth kind of villa was a farmhouse consisting of a large barn with rooms at either end. This was a humbler kind of residence than either the courtyard or the corridor villas.

Britain Under the Romans, by S. E. Winbolt (Penguin Books, 1945)

Roman Britain, by I. A. Richmond (Penguin Books, 1955)

Round Barrow. This is one of the commonest forms of pre-historic monument; round barrows are far more numerous than long barrows. Unlike the latter, which were used for communal burials, each round barrow normally formed the tomb of only one body, although there are examples of round barrows over communal graves.

Round barrows mostly date from the Early and Middle Bronze Ages (1900-1000 B.C.), but there are a few of the Late Bronze Age (1000-450 B.C.). In the earliest round barrows the bodies were buried in a crouched position; but later cremation was carried out and the ashes of the dead persons were placed in urns. Sometimes the urn was surrounded by a ring of posts and occasionally a barrow was built over the dead man's house.

There are various types of round barrow. The earliest was the bowl barrow, which was shaped like a pudding and sur-rounded by a ditch. Later came bell barrows and disk barrows. In the former type there is a level space between the mound and the ditch. The ditch of the disk barrow is its most noticeable feature, for in this kind of barrow the mound is very small. Occasionally double bell barrows and double disk barrows are to be seen. There is another type, known as the pond barrow, which has no mound but is a saucer-shaped depression.

The best place to study barrows is undoubtedly around Stone-henge in Wiltshire. There are three hundred in the locality, including all the types mentioned above.

It is not safe to assume that all mounds date from the Bronze Age, for the Romans and Saxons also occasionally built mounds over tombs.

A Guide to the Prehistoric and Roman Monuments in England and Wales, by Jacquetta Hawkes (Chatto and Windus, 1951)
Britain B.C., by S. E. Winbolt (Penguin Books, 1943)

Round House.   See *Lock-up*

S

Sanctuary.   See *Bronze Age Sanctuary*

Sanctuary Cross, or **Boundary Cross.**   Crosses were sometimes erected to mark the boundary of land owned by monasteries. They also showed the area inside which wrongdoers had the right to claim sanctuary. (See *Frid Stool*.)   Very few sanctuary crosses remain.   At Sharrow, near Ripon, there is the base of one of them; it is now preserved by the National Trust.

Sanctuary Knocker.   The right of sanctuary has been explained in the notes about the *Frid Stool*.   At some churches sanctuary could be claimed by grasping the door knocker of the church. Durham Cathedral retains its sanctuary knocker, which dates from the twelfth century.   It is in the form of a grotesque head with a ring in its mouth.   More than three hundred people used this knocker to claim sanctuary in the sixty years between 1464 and 1524.

Scold's Bridle.   See *Gossip's Bridle*

Scratch Dial.   See *Sundial*

Scratching Stone.   In an attempt to prevent their cattle from damaging fences by scratching their backs against them, some farmers erect upright stones in their fields especially for the cattle to use. Amateur antiquarians have been known to mistake these scratching stones for prehistoric monoliths!

Sexton's Wheel. This was a strange device used in medieval times. It consisted of two iron wheels about three feet in diameter which revolved on a common axle and could be turned in either direction. The wheels were divided by spokes into sections representing the days of the year dedicated to the Madonna. In each section there was a hole with a string fastened into it. A person who wished to keep the Madonna's fast decided on the day on which to observe it by catching hold of a string as the wheel was spun round.

Only two sexton's wheels remain. They are in the churches at Long Stratton in Norfolk and at Yaxley in Suffolk.

Sheep Pond. See *Dew Pond*

Shell Trumpet. In remote hill farms in North Wales the women-folk use a shell trumpet for summoning the men home to meals from their work in the fields. The trumpet is made by cutting the apex from a conch shell.

Signpost. The name ' signpost ' is usually given to a post with several arms indicating the direction to certain places. Actually this is a fingerpost; a signpost is a post which supports a sign, such as an inn sign. Fingerposts were originally erected when most travellers made their journeys on horseback and consequently the arms were at a convenient height to enable their directions to be read by a mounted man. This is much too high for the modern motorist, and most signposts erected now are much shorter.

Silent Clock. People passing by the Mildmay Arms at Winchester often think that the clock on the front of the building has stopped, for its hands always show the time as ten o'clock. A closer inspection reveals that it is not an actual timepiece, but only a clock face painted on the wall.

This unusual feature dates from 1867. Prior to that year many people obtained liquor on short credit, known colloquially then—as now—as ' on tick '. In 1867 this practice was forbidden by Act of Parliament, and as a polite reminder to their customers that credit was no longer available some innkeepers painted a clock face on their inns to show that ' tick has ceased '.

Sparrow-cote. Places provided by house-builders as sites for nesting sparrows are extremely rare. There are eighteen niches, believed to be for this purpose, in the wall of a building at Bath. It has been suggested that they were placed there in order to prevent the birds from damaging the roof.

Staddle Barn. Sometimes near old farmhouses there are barns built on stone toadstools about two or three feet high. These toadstools are called staddles, a word derived from the Anglo-Saxon *stathol*, meaning a support.

The barns were used as granaries, and were built on staddles in order to make them rat-proof. Rats cannot climb upside down, and so are unable to surmount the top stone of the toadstool.

Standing Stone. See *Menhir*

Steelyard. Most market towns used to have a steelyard, a machine for weighing goods such as hay, wool, and hides on which a market toll had to be paid. It was usually fixed to a beam or small cabin overhanging the road and consisted of a pulley and chain on which the load was suspended. One of the very few steelyards still remaining is at Woodbridge in Suffolk; it was capable of weighing a farm wagon complete with its load.

Stepping Stone. The oldest method of crossing streams was at fords. They were followed by stepping stones, placed at a convenient distance apart, so that the walker could cross without getting his feet wet.

Stepping stones still remain, although few of them are in use, for a bridge has generally been erected nearby. There are several sets in the Yorkshire dales; of these, the best known are probably those across the Wharfe at Bolton Abbey. The river is quite wide at this point, and there are over fifty stones. Many of the younger people prefer to use this more adventurous method of crossing the Wharfe rather than the footbridge which stands not far away.

Stile. There are so many different kinds of stiles that it is not possible to mention them all, but most of them fall into one of three categories—step stiles, ladder stiles, and V-stiles. A V-stile is so called because in appearance it is like a narrow V-shaped gap in the fence; it is sometimes known as a squeezer and in Derbyshire it is called ' the fat man's misery '. Wooden stiles are common in the south of England, but in the north and the south-west stone is more frequently used, while Wales has stiles of slate.

Stocks. It is not known when wrongdoers were first placed in the stocks, although it is certain that the Anglo-Saxons used this form of punishment, which did not go out of fashion until the early nineteenth century. The last time it was used appears to have been at Rugby in 1865.

The stocks were usually made of wood, although sometimes they were of iron. They consisted of two boards or pieces of iron with holes in them through which the legs of the culprit were placed, after which the two sections were padlocked together. A seat was provided for the unfortunate offender. Sometimes there were four holes, so that two persons could be accommodated at the same time.

The object of the stocks was to shame the culprit by making him look ridiculous in the eyes of his friends and neighbours. An Act of Parliament passed in 1350 prescribed a period in the stocks for such offenders as drunkards, thieves, unruly apprentices, and tradesmen who gave short measure.

There are still a considerable number of stocks in existence; many of them are in quite a good state of preservation. Some have whipping posts attached. Those at Brading in the Isle of Wight and at Winchcombe in Gloucestershire are particularly noteworthy because they have five holes and seven holes respectively. In each case the odd hole is supposed to have been made for a one-legged man whose misbehaviour frequently caused him to be placed in the stocks.

Another unusual type of stocks can be seen in the churchyard at Colne in Lancashire. They are on wheels, so it appears miscreants were wheeled around the town while undergoing their punishment.

Stone Avenue.   See *Alignment*

Stone Axe Factory.   The New Stone Age people of eastern and southern England obtained the material for their weapons and tools from flint mines (q.v.).   Those of the north and west quarried their material from the hard rocks and made their implements in stone axe factories.   The sites of very few of these have been discovered; they can be distinguished by the litter of unfinished implements near the surface of the ground.   There was an axe factory on Penmaenmawr, a hill in Caernarvonshire.

Stone Circle.   See *Cromlech*

Sundial.   The sundial is one of the oldest methods of telling the time.   It is mentioned in the Old Testament and was used by the ancient Egyptians.

In this country there are a few Saxon sundials; those at Daglingworth in Gloucestershire, at Kirkdale in Yorkshire, and on the old cross at Bewcastle in Cumberland are examples. The Bewcastle sundial dates from 670.   On the Saxon dials the day was usually not divided into twelve hours but into four tides, the space between each pair of marks on the dial representing one tide or three hours.

For centuries there was a sundial marked on the south wall of most churches.   It consisted of a few lines radiating from a central hole, in which a wooden pointer was fixed.   Sometimes instead of hour lines there was a circle of holes in which a movable peg was placed.   When the shadow of the central pointer fell on the peg or on a certain line the people, who possessed no clocks or watches, knew it was time for them to go to church.   These simple timekeepers are known as mass dials or scratch dials.

Some churches have more elaborate sundials on their walls. Most of these were placed there in the eighteenth century.

The wall sundial was followed by the pedestal type, which was erected in the grounds of many country houses until clocks came into common use.

During official summertime sundials are, of course, one hour slow. An exception is a sundial in Pett's Wood, Kent, which was placed there as a memorial to William Willett, the inventor of daylight saving, but of course in winter it is one hour fast.

Actually sundials seldom show the correct time at all, for they show apparent solar time, whereas Greenwich Mean Time is a measure devised by man. There are only four days in each year when these two kinds of time correspond.

The Book of Sundials, by Mrs A. Gatty (4th edition, 1900)

Sundial Window. Stained glass windows incorporating sundials were popular in the seventeenth and eighteenth centuries, but many of them have disappeared. There is a fine one over a door at Nun Appleton Hall, near Tadcaster, Yorkshire. It has a picture of a cupid in the centre panel and representations of the seasons in the corners. It was the work of Henry Gyles, a York glass painter, who lived from 1645 to 1709.

Perhaps more interesting, although certainly not as fine artistically, is a sundial window in the church at Bucklebury, Berks. In the centre of the sundial is a shield bearing a coat of arms and to the left of the shield a fly is painted on the glass. A life-like effect has been achieved by painting the legs and body of the fly on one side of the glass and the wings on the other side. It seems that the artist included the fly as a joke, since no reason has ever been discovered for its presence in the window.

Suspension Bridge. The use of the principle of suspension in constructing bridges is not a modern one, for prehistoric people formed bridges by fastening ropes to tree trunks on either side of the river. The modern type of suspension bridge is thought to have originated in the Indus valley, for a document of the seventh century A.D. tells of the use of iron chains for suspension bridges there.

The first suspension bridge in England, and possibly in Europe, was a footbridge erected across the River Tees near Holwick in 1704. Although the original bridge no longer stands, there is still one on the same site.

In 1820 Sir Samuel Brown erected the first large suspension bridge in England. It was across the Tweed near Berwick. Unfortunately it lasted for only six months, being destroyed in a storm.

Only five years later Thomas Telford completed his masterpiece, the bridge across the Menai Straits, which still stands today and is one of the two finest suspension bridges in the country. The other is Isambard Brunel's bridge across the Avon at Clifton, near Bristol ; this was erected in 1864.

Swing Bridge. In this type of bridge part of the structure turns on a pivot. There are small wooden swing bridges on many canals.

Sword Rest. In churches which were frequently attended by civic dignitaries a receptacle was provided in which they could place their swords during the service. Sword rests can still be seen in the church of St Philip and St James at Bristol.

T

Teazle Tower. Teazles (or teasels)—the spiky heads of the plant *dipsacus fullonum*—were used to raise a ' nap ' on woollen cloth after weaving. Before they could be used they had to be dried. Sometimes towers were built especially for this purpose; they had latticed floors so that a good current of air was provided. The teazles were grown mainly in Devon and Somerset. Very few towers remain; there is one with three storeys at Woodchester in Gloucestershire.

Tethering Post. In some towns and villages iron posts can be found with rings attached to them to which riders fastened their horses while they did their shopping or attended to other business. There are several of these posts in the High Street at Market Harborough in Leicestershire.

Thatched Roof. Despite the widespread use of other roofing materials, the art of thatching still survives. It has changed little during the course of centuries.

The styles of thatching vary in different parts of the country. The material used also varies, because one which is easily available in one locality is rare in another. For this reason rushes are used in Essex, unthreshed straw in Devon, wheat straw in Dorset, and river reed in Norfolk. The latter lasts longer than the other types of thatch and has the further advantage of being much less inflammable. A roof thatched with river reed may need no repairs for fifty years or more.

Before being used for thatching, the straw has to be cleaned and then made wet, otherwise it will not lie smoothly on the roof. This process of cleansing and wetting is known as ' yelming ', and each bundle of clean straw is called a ' yelm '. Five or six bundles form a ' burden ', the amount which can be carried to the roof in a forked stick known as a ' jack '. This is one of the tools of the thatcher's trade, all of which are quite simple, so that most of them are made by the thatcher himself or by the village blacksmith.

Briefly, the process of thatching a new house is as follows: Straw is first sewn on to the rafters until there is a layer at least a foot thick. Then more straw is laid out in a horizontal ' lane ' along the lower part of the roof. This ' lane ' is fastened down with pegs, and more ' lanes ' are made in the same manner, so that each of them overlaps the one below.

The final appearance of the roof depends upon the design favoured by the thatcher. There is quite a variety of patterns used, and it is interesting to count the number of different ones to be seen in the same village.

Tidal Mill. Mills worked by the tide used to be fairly common around the coast. As the tide rose the water was collected in a reservoir, and it started to work the mill after the tide began to fall. The mill could usually continue working for several hours.

In 1938 an inquiry revealed that twenty-three of these mills remained, of which ten were still worked by the tide. Now the working tidal mills appear to be reduced to one—that at Woodbridge in Suffolk.

Tile-hanging. This is the practice of hanging tiles on battens over the upper half of the walls of a house in order to give extra protection. It is common in Sussex, Surrey, and Kent.

Tithe Barn. Tithes used to be paid in kind instead of in cash. For centuries they were the Church's chief source of income. When they were first introduced into England towards the end of the eighth century they were intended to be used for the relief of the poor and the maintenance of the church fabric. Later the priest who collected them was allowed to keep part of them.

Tithe barns were constructed to store the tithes. They were usually large and well built, many of them being over 150 feet long; the length of that at Abbotsbury in Dorset is 276 feet. Most of those which survive are five hundred or six hundred years old. Some of the finest are in Wiltshire and Somerset.

A few tithe barns are still used for various purposes, but not for the storage of tithes. By an Act of Parliament passed in 1836 tithes in kind were commuted into cash. The barn at Stanway in Gloucestershire has been converted into a parish hall, and that at Ashford in Derbyshire is an art gallery.

Tithe Scales. Some churches used to possess scales and a set of weights which were used to measure tithes. The tithes, consisting of a tenth part of the produce or annual value of much of the land in the parish, had to be given each year towards the maintenance of the church and its incumbent. Very few of these scales and weights are still preserved; there are some dated 1795 in the church at Brookland, Kent.

Tollboard. Boards at each end of the few tollbridges or toll roads which exist announce the tolls which modern traffic has to pay. Occasionally one comes across a much older board; there is one at Crickhowell in Breconshire dated 1587.

Toll-house. In the early part of the nineteenth century there were eight thousand tollgates across the roads of England. The stretches of road between these gates had been built by bodies called Turnpike Trusts, who were allowed to collect tolls at the gates from all traffic using the roads. The money collected was supposed to be used to maintain the roads in a good state of repair, but often very little of it was used for that purpose and it went straight into the pockets of the members of the Trust.

The tolls were collected by tollgate keepers, who lived in cottages beside the gates. Although the gates have disappeared, many of the cottages still remain. They are usually built right on the edge of the road, with no garden or pavement between them and the highway. Sometimes they are an unusual shape —round or hexagonal—in order that the windows could look out on all sides and make it difficult for anybody to pass unnoticed. Occasionally somewhat ornate buildings, like miniature castles, were erected, so that travellers who wanted to evade payment of the tolls could not make the excuse that they thought the toll-house was an ordinary cottage. One of these rather elaborate toll-houses is to be seen at Devizes in Wiltshire; it is known as Shane's Castle.

The turnpike trusts gradually went out of existence during the nineteenth century, as responsibility for the maintenance of the roads was transferred to the local authorities. The last trust, which was responsible for a stretch of road in Anglesey, was abolished in 1895.

Town Gate. A number of our older cities still possess one or more of the gates through which all traffic had to pass in the days when the city was surrounded by massive walls for defensive purposes. The Normans built six gates in Canterbury's walls; today only one—the West Gate—remains. Winchester has two of its five gates; the upper part of the Westgate is now a museum.

The narrowness of the roads through some of these old gates has led to traffic problems. Southampton has solved this difficulty by widening its modern High Street at the point where the town's majestic Bar Gate stands, leaving the gate like an island in the middle of the busy thoroughfare.

Town Hall. Most towns have a hall where the borough council or urban district council meet and have their offices. Some of them are of historical or architectural interest; that at Windsor, for example, was finished by Sir Christopher Wren after the death of the architect who had been engaged to supervise the work. Some towns whose population and prosperity have declined until today they are only small villages still retain their old town halls. Newtown in the Isle of Wight, which was once a busy port, is one of these places and its town hall now belongs to the National Trust.

A few buildings erected as town halls are now used for other purposes. The hall at Bradford-on-Avon in Wiltshire was built over a hundred years ago by a group of private citizens and was subsequently acquired by a bank, although the council continued to meet there. The bank sold it and it now provides accommodation for a Roman Catholic church.

Transporter Bridge, or **Aerial Ferry.** This is an unusual type of bridge; there are only three in England. It has a high-level span, so that ships can pass under it all the time. Traffic is carried over the river either on a moving suspended platform or in suspended cars. England's three transporter bridges are at Middlesbrough ; across the Mersey between Widnes and Runcorn; and across the Usk at Newport.

The Widnes-Runcorn bridge is 1,000 feet in length and is the longest bridge of its kind in the world. It is shortly to be replaced by a road bridge.

Tread-Wheel. (Also known as Windlass Wheel, Man Wheel, or Donkey Wheel.)

One of the oldest lifting devices is a wheel so constructed that the weight of a man or animal walking slowly forward is converted into a vertical lifting force. It was used by the Romans and there are still a few in regular use in this country.

The best-known is that at Carisbrooke Castle in the Isle of Wight. This is also the largest power wheel. It is worked by a donkey and is used to lift a bucket from a deep well. When full the bucket weighs 3 cwt.

Other examples are at the Fox and Hounds Inn at Beauworth, Hampshire; Beverley Minster in Yorkshire; and in Canterbury Cathedral. Those at Beverley and Canterbury were used to haul material into the towers for repair.

Triangulation Station, or **Trigonometrical Station.** This is a point from which angle readings are made with a theodolite during the mapping of the country by the Ordnance Survey. It is marked by a small concrete pillar or a cairn, with a metal plate at the top inscribed ' Ordnance Survey Triangulation Station ' and another metal plate near the base holding a bracket at a known height above mean sea level. This bracket is used in levelling operations.

The station owes its name to the fact that in mapping the country is divided into a number of triangles. Only two lines at the beginning and end of the network are actually measured; all the other distances are worked out by trigonometry.

Trilithon. This is a prehistoric work consisting of a stone lintel lying on two upright stones. There are several examples at Stonehenge.

Trompe l'Œil Window, or **Mock Window.** A few houses have fake windows, which seem to have been made for the purpose of giving a decorative appearance to what would otherwise be blank walls. At Stoke Edith in Herefordshire there is a circular house with one of these mock windows. The wooden frame and the glass are real, but the curtains, the blind, and the geraniums consist only of paint.

Tubular Bridge. This is a railway bridge consisting of a long tubular iron beam, through which the trains run. Two of the best-known tubular bridges, the Britannia Bridge across the Menai Straits and the Conway Tubular Bridge, were both built by Robert Stephenson about the middle of the nineteenth century. The Britannia Bridge, which is much the larger, consists of two tubular beams each 1,511 feet long.

The Britannia and Conway Tubular Bridges, by Edwin Clark (1850)

Tumble Gate. See *Gate*

Turf Cutting. See *Hill Figure*

Turf Maze. At a number of places there are mazes formed by the construction of little turf banks. The origin of these mazes is obscure, but most of them appear to have been made by monks. They were probably intended as a means of penance; the wrongdoers had to shuffle on their knees round the winding pathway to the middle of the maze.

It has also been suggested that they may have been a form of amusement rather than punishment, and that the villagers competed against each other to see who could follow the pathway from beginning to end in the shortest time.

Among the places which still possess mazes are Breamore in Hampshire, Wing in Rutland, and Asenby in Yorkshire. That at Breamore is only 79 feet wide, but the path it makes is about half a mile long.

U

Upping Block. See *Mounting Block*

V

Vallum. This word is generally used to describe an earthen bank or rampart erected in prehistoric times, but there is one important exception to this. There is a wide ditch running beside Hadrian's Wall; this ditch is known as the Vallum.

Vamping Horn. In some parishes people were summoned to worship by means of a large horn, called a vamping horn, instead of by ringing church bells. It was often used for other

The fortified bridge at Monmouth

Watch box, Warblington, Hampshire

purposes as well, such as rousing the villagers from bed, and possibly for amplifying the singing of the choir. A vamping horn is preserved in the church at Willoughton in Lincolnshire.

Vertical Lift. See *Canal*

Viaduct. A viaduct is an arched structure by means of which a road or railway is carried over low-lying ground. Railway viaducts are more numerous than road viaducts. There is a fine railway viaduct at Saddleworth in Yorkshire; it is 950 feet long and stands 66 feet above the valley of the Tame. An eleven-arched road viaduct can be seen at Limpley Stoke in Somerset.

Vicarage. See *Fortified Vicarage*

Village Cross. Many of our villages possess ancient crosses. These are usually in a prominent position, often on the village green. Some of these were erected as preaching crosses (q.v.), others as market crosses (q.v.). In the Middle Ages, if a village was more than six miles from a market it could appeal for authority to establish one of its own. When an application was granted, a cross was often erected on the site of the proposed market to commemorate the event. Some villages did not construct a cross especially for this purpose, but made use of an existing preaching cross. Among the villages which possess old crosses are Linby, Nottinghamshire; Steeple Ashton, Wiltshire; Bonsall, Derbyshire; and Middleham, Yorkshire. The cross at Middleham is in two parts, and traders are supposed to have sealed their bargains by shaking hands in the space between them.

Village Hall. Towns and cities have had their town halls and guildhalls for centuries, but the village hall is a comparatively recent type of public building. Because of the small amount of money usually available, few village halls are of architectural interest; in fact, some are plain and even ugly. There are a few which are distinguished from the rest by the beauty of their design or the manner in which their interior decoration has been carried out. A hall notable in both these respects is that at Eastergate in Sussex; it contains twelve fresco paintings by Byam Shaw of scenes from the history of the county.

H

Village Pump. This is a relic of the days when most villagers had to obtain their water from a communal supply. Some of these pumps continue to be in use and London still has one of its old pumps at Aldgate. A small shelter, known as a pump-house, was often erected to protect the pump and those using it from the weather.

Village Sign. In recent years more and more villagers have adopted the pleasant practice of erecting a village sign. A number were set up to mark the last two coronations and the Festival of Britain. Those on the Royal Sandringham estate in Norfolk are much older, for they were erected by King George V in 1912.

One of these, that at Flitcham, depicts the landing of St Felix, a continental missionary who gave his name to the village. (It was called St Felix's Hamlet, but this gradually became changed to Flitcham.) A pictorial representation of the name of the village is a common form of village sign; that at Mayfield in Sussex is a fine example. Other signs depict scenes from village history, as at Cawston in Norfolk, or the village coat of arms, as at Newdigate in Surrey. That at Iver in Bucks shows some of the local scenery. At Bentley, Hampshire, the sign, which was erected by the first Lord Baden-Powell, resembles an open book on which are recorded events in the village's history.

Virgin's Crown. See *Funeral Garland*

Vitrified Fort. This type of fort was built in Scotland by invaders who arrived there during the Early Iron Age. These invaders, known as the La Tène people, came from France. The forts were constructed of rubble, including wood, with stone facings bonded together with timber. It was intended that the materials should remain in that state, but sometimes they caught fire or were set alight by an enemy. It seems that the sockets in which the timbers were fitted acted as flues, and the heat was so great that the stones were melted and fused together. The result was a vitrified fort, such as those found at Finavon in Angus and at Castle Law near Abernethy.

War Bridge. In medieval times some of the larger bridges were fortified, usually by the erection of tower gateways. When conditions became more peaceful nearly all these gateways were removed because they impeded traffic. Today only two fortified bridges remain: Monnow Bridge at Monmouth and Warkworth Bridge in Northumberland.

War Memorial. The crosses and cenotaphs erected to commemorate the dead of the first world war are a familiar sight in towns and villages. In the villages they are usually simple crosses, while in some of the towns they are more elaborate structures, often with statues. Frequently the names of those killed in the second world war have been added.

After the last conflict a more sensible attitude was adopted regarding methods of commemorating the dead. Instead of spending a great deal of money on a useless stone memorial, a large part of it was often spent on some project which would be of benefit to the community, such as a village hall.

A few memorials have been erected to large groups of men. One of these is the fine memorial at Runnymede in Surrey, which commemorates all the airmen of the British Commonwealth who lost their lives and whose graves are unknown. Such memorials as these are designed by famous architects; that at Runnymede was the work of Sir Edward Maufe. The designers of most of the simple village crosses are unknown, although in a few cases great architects were also responsible for these. An example is the cross at Busbridge in Surrey, which was the work of Sir Edwin Lutyens, who also designed London's famous cenotaph in Whitehall.

Occasionally one comes across a memorial of the happy but rare event when all the men of a village or unit returned alive after the first world war. A very interesting example of this type of memorial is at Sledmore in Yorkshire. It commemorates a unit called the Waggoners' Special Reserve. This unit had nearly one thousand members, all of whom survived, although many of them served in the British Expeditionary Force in 1914. The memorial has some fine carvings by Carlo Magnoni.

Watch Box. About a hundred and fifty years ago, when the scientific study of surgery was developing, it was very difficult for medical students to obtain bodies for dissection because of the strong prejudice against this. They therefore resorted to the practice of stealing the bodies of newly-buried persons from their graves during the hours of darkness. Sometimes they did the stealing themselves; at other times they employed rogues known as ' body-snatchers ' or ' resurrection men '. To prevent body-snatching some parishes employed a night-watchman to guard the churchyard and built a small hut for him. There are two of these huts, which were known as watch-boxes, at Warblington in Hampshire.

Watchman's Box. In some English towns and villages the forerunner of the constable was the watchman, who was supposed to see that order was maintained during the hours of darkness. Often one of his duties was to walk around the village and call the hour. Sometimes he was provided with a little hut, known as a watchman's box, with a tiny lock-up attached in which he could imprison anybody who disturbed the peace. The watchman's box at Petersham in Surrey is preserved as an ancient monument.

Water Clock. At Dinnet, in Aberdeenshire, there is a clock worked by water from a hillside spring. The water is made to drip at the rate of sixty drops each minute on to a wooden wheel, which operates the works of the clock. This clock never stops and never needs rewinding. There is another water clock in a hotel at Beaumaris in Anglesey.

Water-mill. When man first used the power of water to grind corn is unknown, but it is certain that there were water-mills in ancient Greece. In A.D. 395 laws were made for the protection of the water-mills in Rome. It was probably the Romans who introduced water-mills to England, although the earliest mention of them in the British Isles is in an Irish poem written early in the eleventh century.

In Norman times they were the only source of power and consequently were listed in the Domesday Book. This record is a valuable one, for if a mill was mentioned in Domesday or was on the site of a Domesday mill, it was exempt from tithes. Consequently we can be fairly sure that the places mentioned in Domesday as having mills continued to possess mills on exactly the same sites for centuries.

The fact that a Domesday site was exempt from tithes was not the main reason for continuing to maintain a mill there. The chief reason was, of course, that which had caused the original mill to be built—the flow of water there was more suitable, or dams to regulate the flow could be constructed more easily, than at any other point in the vicinity.

Sometimes the only part of an old mill that still survives today is the water-wheel. There are a number of different types of water-wheels, the three main ones being known as undershot, overshot, and breast.

The first of these is a wheel whose centre is above the effective level of the stream. The overshot wheel is beneath the level of the water, which usually reaches it from a trough or aqueduct. Instead of paddles, it is fitted with buckets to receive the water. The overshot wheel gets the benefit of the full impulse of the water, but its speed may be retarded to a certain extent because the bottom of the wheel has to move against the current. This difficulty is overcome in the pitch-back overshot wheel, where the direction of the water is reversed before it falls on to the top of the wheel. The breast wheel, like the overshot, is fitted with buckets. It is partly enclosed in a culvert, so that the water reaches it over the top of a sluice at about thirty degrees from the top of the wheel.

Most water-mills are three or four storeys high. Often the

two lower storeys are of stone or brick and the remainder are of timber. A distinctive feature of the exterior of a water-mill is the lucomb. This is a little cabin projecting from the top of the building, the purpose of which was to facilitate the unloading of grain and the loading of flour.

Water-mills were originally erected to grind grain, of course, but a large number were built for other purposes, particularly in the early stages of the Industrial Revolution. Paper, woollen, and cotton mills all used water-power. When the Weald of Surrey and Sussex produced iron, the bellows of the blast furnaces were operated by water-power. Other purposes for which water-mills were used included grinding cement and flint.

Surrey, Kent, Norfolk, Hampshire, Somerset, and Devon possess many water-mills. They also abound in Wales and Scotland, where the mountain streams provide plenty of water-power. In the latter country they were used for tweed-making.

Few of the remaining water-mills are more than three centuries old. In recent years more and more of them have become disused. Now very few indeed still produce flour; if they are used, their work is usually confined to milling corn for animals. Many have been converted into private residences, and sometimes the wheels are used to drive plants to generate electricity.

British Windmills and Watermills, by C. P. Skilton (Collins, 1947)

Old Surrey Watermills, by J. Hillier (Skeffington, 1951)

Wayside Cross. Wayside crosses were sometimes set up for the benefit of travellers. When they reached one of these monuments they gave thanks for having travelled in safety so far and prayed that the remainder of their journey might also be without harm. There is a cross near Great Hatfield in Yorkshire which may have been erected for this purpose.

Wayside Pump. Although stage coaches travelled at only about fifteen miles an hour they often created a great cloud of dust on the roads, which in those days had not the tarmac surface we know today. In an attempt to lessen the dust problem,

Parliament ordered the Turnpike Trusts, which maintained the roads, to erect pumps beside them and use the water for keeping the dust down. There is one of these pumps near Hartley Wintney, in Hampshire, and another on the Bath Road near Newbury in Berkshire.

Weather-boarding. Sometimes long slats of wood are hung on battens around the upper half of a house, in order to give extra protection. In the east of Sussex and in Kent these boards are often painted white and add considerably to the pleasant appearance of the cottages. In Essex, on the other hand, they are sometimes covered with black pitch.

Weathervane. The earliest weathervane may have been the golden Triton holding a rod which surmounted the Tower of the Winds in Athens. This was erected about 50 B.C. Long before that pennants and streamers had been used to indicate the direction of the wind. There were weathercocks in England by the eighth century. In the thirteenth century only noblemen were allowed to have weathervanes.

The oldest weathercock still in use in this country is on the tower of Ottery St Mary church in Devon. It is believed to date from 1335 and is unique in that it actually crows. The crowing sound is made by the wind blowing through two tubes in the body of the cock.

Most of the early English weathervanes were in the form of a banner and did not possess a pointer. The oldest vane of this type is on Etchingham church, Sussex, and was placed there in 1387.

The first buildings in this country to be provided with weathervanes were churches, whose towers and spires formed ideal sites. The choice of a cock to serve as a pointer may have arisen from the fact that it is a symbol of vigilance; it seems strange that quite a number of churches have vanes in the form of a dragon, which to Christians was for centuries the symbol of sin. In the ninth century the Pope decreed that a weathercock must be placed on all church steeples to signify the Church's sovereignty and to remind Christians that they must be vigilant.

Another early Christian symbol found on weathervanes is the fish; the Greek word for fish is formed by the initial letters of 'Jesus Christ, Son of God, Saviour '.

Often there are no cardinal points on church weathervanes. They were not necessary because the nave and chancel stretched from west to east.

A few churches have the privilege of placing a crown over their vanes. One of these is St Martin-in-the-Fields, London, which is the parish church for Buckingham Palace.

Weathervanes of many interesting and varied designs are to be found on public buildings, business premises, and private dwellings. Often they are fine examples of the metalworker's art.

At one time weathervanes were placed on top of telegraph poles, but this practice ceased in 1912 and very few of these poles have survived.

English Weathervanes, by A. Needham (Charles Clarke, 1953)

Weeping Cross. Weeping crosses were sometimes set up in churchyards and beside the routes followed by funeral processions. There were hollows in the base of the cross and at one time it was thought these were knee-holes in which penitents could kneel and pray; now it is believed that they were intended for votive offerings. There is the base of a weeping cross in the churchyard at Ripley in Yorkshire. Weeping crosses were also known as cortège crosses.

Well. In early times many wells had healing powers attributed to them, and today there are still six hundred of these healing springs in Britain. Some of them were also credited with the ability to grant wishes.

Cornwall, where superstition lingered long, seems to have more of these wells than any other part of the country, but the most famous healing well is St Winifred's, at Holywell in Flintshire. This has been a shrine for many centuries, for its waters were supposed to cure a number of ailments. There is a collection there of crutches and other articles discarded by those who were cured by its waters.

The waters of many wells were thought to be effective for the treatment of only one particular type of ailment. Those at Dunsfold in Surrey and at Hope Baggot in Shropshire were believed to be a cure for eye troubles.

Among the more unusual powers attributed to wells were those of ensuring mastery over the household to whichever partner of a marriage was the first to drink of the water after a wedding, and of preserving those baptized in the water from ever being hanged. The first of these powers was supposed to belong to St Keyne's Well, near Liskeard in Cornwall, and the second to the well at Ludgvan in the same county.

Often people desiring a cure or the granting of a wish were expected to make some payment at the well. A pin had to be thrown into St Helen's well at Brindle in Lancashire in order to have a wish granted. A small piece of cheese was the payment demanded at a well between Carlisle and Selkirk, while at others actual money had to be thrown into the waters.

Besides healing wells and wishing wells there were also cursing wells, although these appear to have been far less numerous. There is one at St Elian's in Denbighshire. It was believed that if a pebble on which a person's name had been scratched was thrown into the water, then that person would certainly die.

Whalebone Gate. In some places on the coast of northern Scotland there are gateways formed of the ribs or jawbones of whales. One of these gates can be seen at Bragar on the Isle of Lewis.

Whipping Post. Whipping posts, like the stocks, to which they were often attached, were for centuries a common instrument of punishment. They consisted of wooden posts fitted with iron clamps to which prisoners were tied whilst they received the number of lashes ordered by the justices. Whipping was the punishment for more serious offences than those for which a period in the stocks was decreed.

White Horse. This is by far the commonest type of figure cut in the chalk downlands and seems to have been chosen as a subject for this form of art long before any other symbol. The horse at Uffington in Berkshire, which is believed to have been constructed in the Early Iron Age, is the oldest hill figure still in existence.

There are seventeen white horses and more than half of them are in one county—Wiltshire. The best-known Wiltshire horse is that usually referred to as Westbury White Horse, although it is actually nearer to the village of Bratton than to the town of Westbury. After the Uffington horse, it is the oldest in England, although Scotland's only horse at Mormond in Aberdeenshire may be a few years older. The Westbury horse was constructed in 1778, on the site of an earlier horse.

Nearly all the other horses were cut in the latter part of the eighteenth or during the nineteenth centuries. There are, however, two horses which were made in the present century—at Litlington, Sussex, and Pewsey, Wiltshire. Only one horse—that at Osmington in Dorset—has a rider.

Most of the horses appear to have been constructed merely with a view to making some addition to the landscape, although one or two were made for commemorative purposes.

The horses vary considerably in size. The Uffington animal, besides being the oldest, is also the largest; it is about 360 feet long. The smallest, less than 30 feet long, is near Stockbridge in Hampshire.

White Horses and Other Hill Figures, by Morris Marples (Country Life, 1949)

Winchester Bushel. Weights and measures used to be based on standards kept at Winchester. Many places had a bushel measure, known as a Winchester bushel, which was used in connection with the tithe grain; one is preserved in the church at Hingham in Norfolk.

Windlass Wheel. See *Tread-wheel*

Windmill. There are three main types of windmill. The oldest is the post mill, in which the structure pivots on a central post. In all windmills some arrangement is necessary to enable the sails to be turned round to face the wind; in the case of the post mill the entire mill had to be turned. The miller did this by pushing on a long beam which projected from the back of the mill. There is a post mill dating from 1668 at Brill in Buckinghamshire.

In the tower mill it is not necessary for the whole structure to be turned, because the sails are fixed to a cap or gable. This is turned, while the rest of the building remains stationary. In the earliest kind of tower mill the cap was turned by means of a long tail-pole. The largest tower mill still standing is at Sutton in Norfolk; it is nearly 80 feet high. Tower mills are built of brick, and are usually round.

The third type of mill, the smock mill, is covered with boards and is generally octagonal. As in the tower mill, only the cap revolves. The finest smock mill in England is at Cranbrook in Kent; it was built in 1814.

Until 1745 the miller had to turn the mill or the cap by hand to ensure that the sails were facing into the wind. Then the invention of the fantail enabled the wind to do this work in addition to making the sails revolve. A fantail is a miniature windmill set at right-angles to the main structure. It remains stationary as long as the sails face the wind, but when the wind changes the fantail is set in motion and turns the mill or its cap round until the sails can again take full advantage of the wind.

Variations in the wind also make it necessary to adjust the area of sail. In the earliest mills this had to be done by hand; the sails, which each consisted of a large sheet of cloth spread over a wooden framework, had to be stopped while the miller climbed on to each one of them and furled or unfurled the cloth. This was a difficult and dangerous task. In 1772 the spring sail was invented. This was formed of hinged shutters of wood or canvas on a wooden framework, something like a venetian blind. The shutters were opened or closed by means of a long bar, to which they were all connected. This was a great achievement, since the miller no longer had to climb on the sails, although they still had to be stopped in order that the adjustment could be made. The patent sail, invented in 1807, had a device whereby all the connecting bars were linked to a striking rod and a mechanism enabled the wind to open and close the shutters, so that it was no longer necessary to stop the mill.

Most windmills have four sails, but there are also mills with five, six, or eight sails. The eight-sailed mill at Heckington in Lincolnshire has been preserved by the Kesteven County Council. There were also one or two mills with an annular, or ring-shaped, sail.

The axle which carries the sails is known as the windshaft. Fixed to it inside the body of the mill is the brake wheel, which is so called because the sails can be stopped by the action of a brake on it. By means of cog-wheels, the upright shaft which runs vertically through the centre of the body of the mill is made to revolve, and this turns the stones which grind the corn. There are three main sources of these stones—Derbyshire, France, and Germany.

Most windmills were used to grind corn, although a large number in East Anglia were erected as drainage mills. The drainage mill at Berney Arms in Norfolk served a double purpose—it was also used to grind cement clinker. Other purposes for which windmills were used included sawing wood and grinding chalk, ochre, white lead, bark, and snuff.

Norfolk, Suffolk, Kent, Sussex, Lincolnshire, Cambridge-shire and Lancashire are the English counties where windmills were fairly common. Wales had few windmills; there are a number of disused ones on Anglesey. In Scotland windmills were very rare, although Edinburgh possessed one up to the seventeenth century.

During the present century the windmill has become a com-paratively rare feature of the English landscape, after being prominent for seven hundred years. The earliest written refer-ence to a windmill in this country is dated 1191, and the earliest illustration of one is in a psalter of 1270. This is a picture of a post mill; the first illustration of a tower mill is in a French manuscript of 1420. The oldest post mill still in existence is at Bourn in Cambridgeshire; it was erected more than three hundred years ago.

The decline of the windmill began with the invention of the steam engine. The windmills of the countryside lost their trade to mills driven by steam power in the towns. Then the increasing importation of grain from abroad led to the erection of huge mills at the ports. Now there are only about twenty windmills left which still work by wind.

> *The English Windmill*, by Rex Wailes (Routledge and Kegan Paul, 1954)
>
> *British Windmills and Watermills*, by C. P. Skilton (Collins, 1947)
>
> *Windmills in England, a study of their origin, development, and future*, by Rex Wailes (Architectural Press, 1948)

Wishing Well. See *Well*

Witch's Stone. This is a large block of granite which recalls an old Scottish custom. A woman who was believed to be a witch was placed in a barrel through which spikes were driven and the barrel was then rolled down a hill. When it came to rest, the barrel and all that remained of the poor woman were covered with tar and burned and a boulder, known as a witch's stone, was placed on the spot where the burning took place. There is a witch's stone near Forres in Moray.

Y

Youth Hostel. A green triangle bearing the letters *YHA* indicates that the building with this sign is a youth hostel. The youth hostel movement began in Germany in 1910, when a schoolmaster, Robert Schirrmann, opened a hostel where school-children and young people could stay during holidays spent in walking.

Nearly twenty years passed before the idea spread to this country. In 1928 the Northumbrian Trampers' Guild provided six ' shelters ' for walkers; one of these was later to become the first hostel in Northumberland. Other groups of people were at the same time thinking on somewhat similar lines. The British Youth Council set up a committee to consider the matter, and so did the Ramblers' Association in Liverpool.

It was at Liverpool that the hostelling movement in this country really began, for towards the end of 1929 the Mersey-side Centre of the British Youth Hostels Association was formed. In April of the following year the National Council of Social Service called a conference of interested organizations and it was decided to form the British Youth Hostels Association.

At the end of 1930 the Association's membership was only 170, and no hostel had yet been opened. The association had a national office—a discarded army hut—at Welwyn Garden City. What was much more important, it had an enthusiastic secretary, Mr E. St John Catchpool. Regional Councils were established, Groups were set up in various towns, and public appeals were made for funds.

Early in 1931 twelve hostels were opened. By the end of that year there were seventy-three hostels, and the Association's membership was over six thousand. In the same year the Scottish Youth Hostels Association was established and opened its first hostel.

From those small beginnings the movement has grown, and today the Youth Hostels Association of England and Wales has about three hundred hostels and a hundred and eighty thousand members. These members are entitled to use the hostels in any of the many other countries which belong to the International Youth Hostel Federation.

The hostels vary considerably in size and type. Some can

accommodate more than a hundred people while others have beds for less than twenty. A few have been specially built as hostels, others are converted castles, cottages, mills, or mansions. Much of the task of conversion and many of the repairs are carried out voluntarily by enthusiastic hostellers.

The accommodation and equipment provided are usually quite simple. The hostellers sleep in dormitories and there is a dining-room and a common-room, where they can read or play games. At most hostels meals are provided and there are usually also cooking facilities for use by members who prefer to cook their own food. Each hosteller is expected to perform some simple task, such as sweeping a room or peeling potatoes.

Youth Hostel Story, by Oliver Coburn (The National Council of Social Service, 1950)

Z

Zoological Garden, or **Zoo.** It is believed that there was a zoo in China about 1100 B.C. and it is certain that several of the Pharaohs of Egypt had zoos in the fourth century B.C. England's first zoo was probably the menagerie which Henry I established at the royal palace at Woodstock in Oxfordshire. About fifty years after being founded it was removed to the Tower of London, where it remained until 1834.

A few other zoos were established by the nobility, but the purpose of all of them was merely to amuse and entertain their owners and their owners' friends. It was not until the nineteenth century that zoos were founded as a means of education. In 1828 the Zoological Society opened its famous gardens in Regent's Park in London. This was the first zoo to be owned by a society instead of by a wealthy individual.

In most zoos the animals live in cages. At the zoo at Whipsnade in Bedfordshire, which was opened in 1931, they are given much more freedom, for they roam about in large paddocks.

Other well-known zoos are at Clifton near Bristol; Belle Vue, Manchester; and Chessington in Surrey. One of the most recently established zoos is at Upton, near Chester; it belongs to the North of England Zoological Society, which was formed in 1934.